Sidney,

Thanks for your
dedication to AUS
and your company site
and most importantly,
your country!

Best Regards,

Praise for **Steve Jones** and *No Off Season*

Steve Jones is a world-class chief executive. He has his eyes firmly on serving customers to the best of his ability and on growing his company at a sustainable but rapid pace. He has boundless energy and he never has an off day, let alone an off season.

—MIKE GRAFF
Managing Director, Warburg Pincus
Former Partner, McKinsey & Company
Former Chief Operating Officer, Bombardier Aerospace

Those of us who have lived within the game of football understand it as a template for building a rewarding life. Here, in his terrific book, *No Off Season*, Steve breaks down these football fundamentals into powerful life lessons that anyone can apply to improve their own level of success in business and in life.

—COACH CHUCK PAGANO
Head Coach, Indianapolis Colts (2012–2017)
NFL Defensive Coordinator/Coach (2001–2011)

Steve Jones has done all of us former Cal Poly Mustangs proud with his meteoric rise to the very top of business today. *No Off Season* is a great book in which Steve sets out just how he achieved his tremendous success by living according to the core values that he learned out on the football field. This is a necessary read for anyone interested in developing a winning attitude in business and life.

—COACH TED TOLLNER
Head Coach/Offensive Coordinator, USC (1982–1986)
Head Coach, San Diego State University (1994–2001)
NFL Offensive Coordinator/Asst. Coach (1987–94/2002–10)

Steve Jones has excelled in all aspects of his life and provides a real-life playbook for success. A must read for all who aspire to be their best.

—TIM WALSH
Head Football Coach, California Polytechnic State University Mustangs
(2009-Present)

Having been honored to observe, firsthand, our nation's leaders in combat and in the most senior levels of government, Steve Jones personifies the best. From rough and ready of emergency operations to the highest level of strategic investment, Steve is steely eyed and committed. His ever-growing team of employees know who their coach is and follow like the champions he demands them to be.

—ADMIRAL ROBERT J. NATTER
US Navy Retired Former Commander, US Fleet Forces

No Off Season is deeply impactful. It overflows with dynamic principals applicable in business, sports, and in life. This book increased my commitment to lead the next generation, and it inspired and equipped me to do it.

—A.C. GREEN
Three-time NBA National Champion
Holder of NBA Iron Man Streak at 1,192 straight games (1997–Present)

I came away from my first meeting with Steve Jones not only impressed by his energy, intellect, and business acumen, but also with the impression that he might well have been one of the most capable CEOs with whom I had ever done business. Since that time, my admiration for Steve has only grown as he has demonstrated time and again that he is an inspirational leader, a brilliant businessman, and a man of exemplary character.

—BRETT WHITE
Chairman and CEO, Cushman & Wakefield
Former Chief Executive Officer and President, CBRE Services, Inc.

NO OFF SEASON

NO OFF SEASON

The Constant Pursuit of **More.**

A PLAYBOOK FOR

ACHIEVING MORE IN BUSINESS AND LIFE

STEVE JONES

ForbesBooks

Published by ForbesBooks, Charleston, South Carolina.
Member of Advantage Media Group.

ForbesBooks is a registered trademark, and the ForbesBooks colophon is a trademark of Forbes Media, LLC.

Printed in the United States of America.

10 9 8 7 6 5 4 3 2 1

ISBN: 978-1-94-663350-7
LCCN: 2018956350

Cover design by Brenda Valdez.
Jacket design by George Stevens.
Layout design by Melanie Cloth.

This publication is designed to provide accurate and authoritative information in regard to the subject matter covered. It is sold with the understanding that the publisher is not engaged in rendering legal, accounting, or other professional services. If legal advice or other expert assistance is required, the services of a competent professional person should be sought.

Advantage Media Group is proud to be a part of the Tree Neutral® program. Tree Neutral offsets the number of trees consumed in the production and printing of this book by taking proactive steps such as planting trees in direct proportion to the number of trees used to print books. To learn more about Tree Neutral, please visit **www.treeneutral.com**.

Since 1917, the Forbes mission has remained constant. Global Champions of Entrepreneurial Capitalism. ForbesBooks exists to further that aim by bringing the Stories, Passion, and Knowledge of top thought leaders to the forefront. ForbesBooks brings you The Best in Business. To be considered for publication, please visit **www.forbesbooks.com**.

Like everything else that I do, this book is for my sons,
Carter and Caden:

May you both have the vision to dream big,
the dedication to make those big dreams come true,
and the courage to drive beyond even your greatest successes
so that you can dream something bigger even still.

And may you both know that I will love and support you.
Always.

TABLE OF CONTENTS

Foreword xiii

Acknowledgments xvii

Introduction 1

1. Work 3

2. Hustle 9

3. Do Something 13

4. Put Your Ego in Your Pocket 17

5. Don't Give Up 23

6. Be Kind 29

7. Mentor 33

8. No Excuses (Or Complaints) 39

9. Stand on Your Own 45

10. Adapt 51

11. Accept the Facts 55

12. Endure the Hardships 65

13. Start Early 69

14. Do What You Love 73

15. Find Your Reason 77

16. Get an Ownership Interest 81

17. Check the Boxes 85

18. Follow That Dream 89

19. Don't Look Back 91

20. Take the Risk, But Don't Gamble 95

21. Get Ready to Run 101

22. Don't Cry 111

23. Work Out the Details 121

24. Just Grind 129

25. 9/11 137

26. Rise to the Occasion 141

27. Prepare for Success 147

28. Find A Way 149

29. Follow Your Gut 157

30. Find A Solution 163

31. Go Shopping 167

32. Hire the Best 171

33. Go, Go, Go! 175

34. Make Good on The Dream 181

35. Be a Legend 189

36. You Can Never Have Too Many Partners 195

37. Manage Your Expectations 199

38. Make the Tough Decisions 201

39. Be the Leader 205

40. Move Forward 215

41. Don't Slow Down 219

Conclusion: No Off Season 223

FOREWORD

As a sports attorney and founder of one of professional sports' top representation firms, I suppose it's only logical that there are many people out there who think that our business is simply recruiting and representing some of the top talent currently playing in the NFL and MLB. It's true that our client roster contains many of the most elite players in professional football and baseball, but I see our overall mission as something far greater.

- We are REP 1 Sports and our business is *excellence*.

- Excellence is a concept that is too often misunderstood.

- Excellence is more than simply being very good at whatever your particular pursuit may be. Or even being among the best in the world.

- It is not a static status.

- Excellence is not only the relentless pursuit of being better than the competition, it is the daily dedication to constantly strive to outperform yourself and exceed even the loftiest of goals you might have set for yourself.

That is the fire that drives me, and that is the unique quality that I immediately recognized in Steve Jones. Our initial meeting was while working out at a fitness club in Southern California, and we quickly realized that we shared much in common.

To begin with, we both share a love for the game of football. By that, I don't mean that we are simply fans of the sport, but rather that we understand all of its wonderful complexities and how participation in the game changes you, molds you, and provides you with the skills to go out into the world and achieve.

Our conversations led us to discover that we were also both a part of the Cal Poly football family. While Steve played for the Mustangs, my father, Ted Tollner, was the quarterback for the 1960 squad that was aboard the charter flight that crashed outside of Toledo, killing twenty-two of my dad's friends and teammates.

Steve and I are both aware of the commitment, dedication, and resiliency required in order to take a business and then grow and develop it to its greatest potential.

Yet despite his innumerable personal achievements and all of the business success that Steve has amassed, what I respect most about Steve is his absolute devotion to his wife and sons. While the two of us certainly share that burning passion to achieve on all levels, the commonality that connects us most closely is a shared belief in the resolute importance and value of family.

Having written a number of books, including *The New York Times* bestseller *On the Clock*, I have always been mindful of the need for an author to create something that no one else could offer to their readership. Here, with what I am sure will be the first of many books on business, family, and life, Steve Jones does exactly what I would expect him to do: he absolutely shatters all reasonable expectations.

Within these pages you will find not only an incredible human story, but also the fundamental business principles and life lessons that anyone could need to create a life of meaning and enormous returns—all of it told in the powerful way that only Steve Jones could.

So, without further delay or discussion, it is my pleasure to introduce a man who needs no introduction. The hard-hitting, never-quitting, business giant and man among men, my friend: Steve Jones, a man who truly knows no off-season.

—Bruce A. Tollner, Esq.

ACKNOWLEDGMENTS

I am, by any metric, a fortunate man, but my greatest riches have really come in the form of all of the amazing people who have shaped my life in more ways than I could ever fully address, even in the pages of this book. Still, there were some individuals and organizations that have had a particularly profound impact on me and I would be remiss if I did not call them out and express my deep gratitude.

Any thanks on my part must necessarily begin at the beginning. My father, Steve Jones, was my coach, harshest critic, confidante, life-guide, ass-kicker (when I needed it), and best friend. He instilled in me a burning need to demand the best of myself, a ferocious work ethic, and an unshakable confidence in my ability to realize whatever dream I set my mind to. The success that I have achieved in business is a testament to his legacy, but I am most grateful of all for the blueprint he gave me for being a great father and by watching the joy that he gets by being the best grandfather I have ever seen, never missing a game and always supporting my boys.

My mother, Gail Jones, was my greatest supporter, whether that was sitting in the stands on all of those Friday nights and Saturday afternoons or whether it was the quiet moments we shared in which she offered me her unconditional love and unwavering faith. It would be no exaggeration to say that I simply would not be the man that I am today without her presence in my life.

Thanks, too, to my brother, Jeffery Jones. I understand it's often hard to be the little brother, but he has always made me incredibly proud of the courage he's demonstrated in pursuing his own dreams on his own terms.

Football has played an enormous role in shaping my life and I feel the need to thank all of my friends and teammates, my brothers-in-arms, who have put on pads and helmets and taken the field with me from elementary school right through college ball. In that same way, I am grateful to all of the coaches who led me out onto those fields and taught me the life lessons that the game offers.

I have had the great fortune of finding mentorship in a number of individuals who were generous enough to share their knowledge and experience with me, but I need to make special mention here of Dave Roberson for always being there for me in extraordinary ways. I will always aspire to meet the standard that he set for me.

Over the course of my early career, I had the opportunity to work for and with some truly amazing individuals and to receive some fantastic training and professional development that played an enormous part in shaping my outlook on business and life. I was fortunate to have a number of managers who had the faith in me to allow me opportunities to prove myself and I will always be grateful to them for that support.

The original owners of Universal Protection Service, Stephen Salyer and Jim Moses, brought me aboard and offered me the opportunity of a lifetime—more than once. Of all my many accomplishments in business, there are few that I personally treasure more than the fact that so much of what was transacted between us was done on little more than a handshake, a rare thing in the world today and an even rarer thing in business. They are both gentlemen of their word and I have enormous respect for them both.

Brian Cescolini and I were business partners for more than twenty years, and in that time we achieved a level of success that is simply unparalleled in our industry. Through all of the challenges that we faced together, Brian never lost faith in my vision and always allowed me to dream big ... and then even bigger. I treasure his friendship and look forward to proudly continuing the legacy that he and I built together.

Every business is dependent upon relationships and I want to take this opportunity to thank each and every one of our clients over the years who have extended to us the opportunity to provide them with the best security services in the industry. Many of you have become personal friends and have helped me in so many ways, both professionally and personally. I understand the enormous level of trust that our customers show us by allowing us to protect their businesses and I truly appreciate each and every one of them.

Over the course of our ascendency, we have participated in the acquisition of fifty-eight security companies (and counting.) While business can often be coldly reduced to facts and figures, I want the founders and leaders of every one of those companies to know that I understand the unwritten responsibility in assuming their lifework. I consider them all as contributors to this growing business and I look forward to continuing their legacy with the same level of integrity and customer dedication that they did.

A business is a team. I have been fortunate to lead the very best. I want to thank all of the employees who have bought into my vision and who consistently delivered on the promise that I have made to our clients and our financial partners. Our sales team has earned an unprecedented track record in growing the business organically, from the business development representatives in the field to the leaders who drive the overall program, you're the best in the industry. Our client and operations teams, headed up by incredibly dedicated managers throughout North America and a leadership team that is the best in breed, thanks for keeping the lifeblood of our company pumping. Our back-office team that handles everything from human resources, recruiting and training, accounting and finance, IT, and legal, you are the unsung heroes of our company, always ensuring that we deliver on the promises we make to the more than 210,000 employees we have in the field and to the more than 15,000 customers we have across North America. Our acquisitions team ran at an unprecedented pace and has quite simply changed the industry forever and there is no better group in our industry and the leader of our acquisitions team is a world class deal machine who has truly helped transform our company. And lastly, to our executive leadership team, you have always demonstrated exemplary talent, dedication, and a tireless commitment to our shared vision. You are all in a class by yourselves, and together we have all accomplished something that has never been done before in our industry and I am incredibly proud and appreciative of each and every individual who has contributed to this achievement. I look forward to leading us all into the future and I know we will continue to surpass all expectations and achieve great things.

No business succeeds without financial partners and I have enjoyed the opportunity to work with the very best. Through challenges and triumphs alike, I have found in them not just financiers, but trusted business advisors and treasured friends. Over the years, they have shown an enormous level of trust and faith in me and they have provided the funding that was necessary to feed my dream and grow this business. The individuals know who they are, but I will be forever thankful to Caltius Capital Management, Partners Group, Warburg Pincus, Wendel, and Crescent Capital for the essential roles that they played.

Writing *No Off Season* was a new and exciting experience for me and I need to thank my assistant, Sarah Ellwood, for coordinating my crazy schedule. Shalani Maline was my eyes on this project and I thank her for all of the editorial advice. And thanks to Eyre Price for his help in putting my story on these pages, spending countless nights and weekends with me putting my words to paper. So, thank you, Eyre, for literally working around my crazy schedule.

The biggest thanks of all must be reserved for the person who supports and contributes to my success each and every day, my wife, Stacy. She has been my partner through all of the insane work hours and back-breaking stress that is an unavoidable part of this business. She has always been encouraging of everything I had to do to create Allied-Universal, she provided the foundation for our family so that I could build the foundation for the business. Her unwavering love and support allows me to run harder each and every day.

And a final word of thanks to my sons, Carter and Caden, who make me proud every day and inspire me in a thousand ways. You are both so much more talented than I ever was and I am so excited to watch you each pursue your life's dreams. Nothing is out of reach!

INTRODUCTION

Before we get started, I want to get one thing straight.

This is not a vanity project.

I have zero problems with those whose interests lead them in that direction, but I've never played for public recognition or glory and that's not my motivation in putting my life in print.

Not at all.

At the same time, no amount of humility will obscure the fact that I have made an extraordinary life for myself and realized a level of success that a lot of people aspire to, but only a handful ever actually bring to fruition.

And *that* is my motivation in putting my life to paper.

I am not special. I wasn't blessed at birth with any once-in-a-generation talents. And I certainly wasn't offered any special bargains along the way.

Instead, I achieved my success the only way that I knew how. The same exact way I continue to do it today.

It's not a complicated system taken from a business school curriculum, nor is it a too-easy-to-be-true New Age scheme.

Still, it's my hope that by setting out just exactly how I accomplished everything that I have achieved in my life (and still going stronger than ever) that I might be able to reach out to all of those who share the same sort of goals I've held since childhood and inspire them to make their own ambitions come true by providing them with a blueprint for turning their dreams into reality.

And so that's what you hold in your hands right now.

A roadmap.

A playbook.

Not my life story, that's only anecdotal context to the essential life lessons that I have learned along the way and incorporated into my personal methodology. What you possess between the covers here is everything you need to go out there and make your life what you want it to be.

Good luck.

CHAPTER 1
Work

The American Dream.

If you asked every person in these United States to describe their vision of the American Dream and then compiled all of the many responses you received together into one shared vision, all of those varied voices would go a long way to describing Livermore, California.

The place has a strong blue-collar ethic, surrounded by ranches and what they call vineyards, but which are more like farms than the fancier operations to be found off to the north in the Napa Valley.

People work for a living.

At the same time, since it is home to the Lawrence Livermore National Laboratory and it's relatively close to San Francisco (an hour to the east "as the crow flies"/Who-knows-how-long on the 580), Livermore also attracts a cultured and educated element, as well. There is a respectable commitment to the arts and the schools are generally excellent.

Livermore is ... well, the American Dream.

I should know because I was born right in the heart of it all during in the spring of 1969.

My family was solidly middle class at a time when that still meant something.

My dad, Steve, worked for Aramark, one of the nation's leading uniform and workplace supply services, driving a delivery truck and making commercial sales.

My mom, Gail, had been a flight attendant for TWA, but got grounded when I came along, and transitioned to the role of housewife like most other women at that time and *all* of the women in our neighborhood.

Both my parents worked hard for everything we had and while that might not have been a luxurious life by today's standards of Kardashians and Hiltons, we had everything we needed. And—more than that—we were grateful for everything that we had.

Our house was like most of the other houses in town but came with the extra bonus of a pool in the backyard.

We had a station wagon—wood paneling on the side, the works—and we'd pack it up on summer weekends and head off to the lakes for a camping vacation.

I had a bike.

My dad visited the casinos at Lake Tahoe every once in a while and on one of these occasions, he took his winnings and bought me a bike. A badass BMX racer.

Coolest bike on the block.

Coolest bike on the planet.

I rode that bike everywhere.

To the local mini-mart.

To the park with my friends.

But mostly I rode it to and from practice and games.

Soccer. Wrestling. Baseball. Basketball.

And, my personal favorite, football.

The Jones household was obsessed with sports.

Looking back on it now, I think there were a couple of reasons for that preoccupation.

The first was just that we were good at them.

My dad had played football at the University of Alabama under the great Bear Bryant, but left when the Pittsburgh Pirates signed him to a pro contract. Sports at a very elite level wasn't the stuff of fanboy fantasies in our house, it was the stuff of everyday expectations.

The second (and maybe more important) reason that all of the Jones men were so hyper-focused on sports was that, I think, those pursuits provided a necessary distraction from some of the darker thoughts that plagued so many American men in those days.

My dad's baseball career ended when he was drafted and sent to Vietnam. He never talked much about what happened half a world away, but even as a kid I was aware that there was a shadow of those experiences always cast behind him, tethering him to memories he wanted to lose.

I suppose that this was a curse (or birthright) he inherited from his own father, who had been career Army and had dragged my dad around the world as he rose to the rank of Sergeant Major, the highest rank for a noncommissioned officer (NCO). My grandfather was at the Pearl Harbor Naval Base on the morning of December 7, 1941, and, after that infamous day, he spent the next four years in combat. Those experiences made him tough-as-nails as a man and (I'm sorry to say for the kid who grew up to be my old man) as a father, as well.

So, I think sports gave the Jones men something positive for them to focus their thoughts on when those darker memories of war started to seep into their waking consciousness.

More than that, I think sports gave my father and grandfather a way to bond with one another—and with me—that didn't necessarily require the sorts of deeper emotions that they had each lost along the way.

And sports certainly offered both of them an outlet for their latent militaristic instincts.

When I say militaristic, I mean just that.

There's no qualifier or context there.

My dad was the coach of my Little League team when I was growing up, and he ran that collection of young boys like they were a Big League team in a tight pennant race and it was always late September.

Those boys who missed a practice because they'd spent the day swimming or, God forbid, had been off on a family vacation rode the bench for the next game.

Kids who didn't wear their uniform properly got fined. (Yes, fined. And I promise you that every last one of those fines got paid!)

My friends would flash me a "What the—?" look when that sort of *Full Metal Jacket* discipline was imposed, but I would just shrug my shoulders and look away, because I didn't want to get benched myself. Or fined.

We shagged flies and fielded grounders. Over and over.

We took batting practice till the sun went down and then ran bases until even my dad figured we'd had enough.

Over and over.

Until everything was perfect.

If that tireless work ethic wasn't the most important lesson I ever learned, then it was certainly right up there among them.

Whatever you want to accomplish in this life, whether that's learning how to hit a fastball or to speak a foreign language or to pursue a certain profession, you probably won't be very good at this endeavor when you're first introduced.

(And even if you do have some innate talent, that'll only get you so far. Trust me. It's a fact.)

The fundamental principle behind developing any skill is simply to put in the work.

Over and over again, until it's perfect.

Until you can do it in your sleep.

And then to keep on doing it some more.

I have no hesitation in admitting that I've almost never been the most talented guy on the field—or in the workplace.

I'm fine with that, because I'm always the hardest working guy.

It's simple: win or lose, I will never let myself be outworked by anyone.

I have always come to every game I ever played—and to every negotiation, too—as the guy who worked the hardest to get himself ready for the action to begin.

That would be the first lesson I'd pass along: work.

Whatever you're trying to accomplish: work.

Then, work even harder.

Stay at it until you're absolutely certain you can't do anymore.

And then work some more.

It's in *that* moment, that horrible-wonder-ful-transcendent moment when you've proven your estimation of your limits to be completely false and you've pushed yourself beyond what others are willing to do, that you will finally be able to access that special zone where success is really achieved.

It's in *that* moment, that horrible-wonderful-transcendent moment when you've proven your estimation of your limits to be completely false and you've pushed yourself beyond what others are willing to do, that you will finally be able to access that special zone where success is really achieved.

That's where the game is won or lost.

Where the deal is made.

Everything else is just following through.

CHAPTER 2
Hustle

Since my father grew up on military bases all over the world, you might think that those childhood experiences left him with a memory of exotic tales from faraway lands—and, I suppose, they might have—but mainly what I heard were stories about the difficulties of that upbringing, particularly the financial hardships that their family lived with continually.

My father was always an enterprising guy and even as a child he had no shortage of entrepreneurial spunk. Somehow he got his hands on a shoeshine kit and he'd go around whatever base they happened to be at, offering to shine the soldiers' shoes for a nickel or a dime.

He told me that on a good day he could make five bucks.

On a great one, ten.

I think my father intended his stories to convince me how easy I had it in life, but I just heard them as a series of challenges. And I was certain I could beat my old man.

So, nothing would do but that on the next weekend, we went down to the local hardware store and my father got everything he needed to make me my own shoeshine box—complete with the footrest and everything. It was perfect.

The Old Pro taught me how to shine a pair of shoes the *right* way and then let me practice and practice until I had the technique down pat (which means I shined my dad's shoes for free for a couple of weeks.)

When I felt certain I was ready, my dad gave me a ride to downtown Livermore. There wasn't really a business district or a row of high-end restaurants where there might be a parade of gentlemen looking for a shine on their shoes, so I settled for the local Coco's restaurant.

My dad dropped me there on the sidewalk just outside.

I stayed there all by myself from lunchtime until the sun was starting to set and my dad pulled up to the curb to collect me. But for the hours in between, I asked every guy who passed if they wanted their shoes shined.

I didn't care if they were wearing cordovans, wingtips, or Converse hi-tops.

If they were walking, I was pitching.

"Shine your shoes, mister?"

"Put a shine on those shoes?"

Most just kept walking without so much as acknowledging me. Some gave the kid a smile and a kind word.

But there were a handful of guys who took the time to put a shine on their shoes, a smile on my face, and a dollar in my coffee can cash register.

At the end of the day, that coffee can didn't hold a fortune, but I was certain that there was way more than what my father had been bragging about. And I didn't buy into any of that "inflation-*blah-blah-blah*" or "by today's dollar" nonsense that he gave me all the way home. I knew I'd won the Battle of the Shoeshines.

I was seven years old.

I guess you could say that I've been out there hustling every day since. And that, more than almost anything else, accounts for the success that I have been able to achieve in my life: I'm out there hustling. Every day.

Opportunities abound for those who are willing to put in the work and take the risks.

My day on the street outside of Coco's obviously wasn't the beginning of a shoe shining empire for me.

Still, I had listened to what others were saying about a particular business that they had explored, I'd considered their comments carefully, interjected my own vision into the proposition, and then took the risk to determine how I might improve upon their experiences and returns.

Forget getting your fancy MBA, *that's* the fundamentals of business in the Western world, right there.

The secret is that in order to produce results, even the most enlightened thoughts need to be put into practice.

Almost every day I come across an individual who has a "genius idea" for this or a "revolutionary new take" on that. Most often, I don't think that they're nearly as impressive as they do, but occasionally I get surprised. And I always wonder why they're not doing something more to bring their vision to fruition other than just talking about it to me.

It is never too early to start your kids' business education or to begin to develop the fundamental principles and work ethics that will serve them well for the entirety of their lives.

Get out in the world.

Build your "shoeshine box"—whatever that might be for you.

Take it to Coco's.

Do something.

You might be surprised at the results.

I can certainly guarantee you that whether or not you manage to stuff that coffee can full of bills, you will certainly learn something from the experience.

On that note, while my primary focus here is obviously addressing the host of adult issues regularly confronted in the marketplace and preparing oneself for success, I think there's a more family-oriented takeaway to be had here, as well. Specifically, it is never too early to start your kids' business education or to begin to develop the fundamental principles and work ethics that will serve them well for the entirety of their lives.

In this day and age, I certainly can't endorse leaving your seven-year-old on the city sidewalks to make their hustle shining shoes, but those concerns aside, there's no reason that children can't be introduced to these concepts and practices at an early age.

CHAPTER 3
Do Something

Sports were very much the foundation of my childhood.

I played them all. And, I must admit, I was good at them all, too.

Still, football was more than just a sport to me.

Football was my love. I played it every chance I got.

I was very lucky that my elementary school had its own football team, a real team that was part of a real conference with scheduled games and everything.

As a fifth grader, I saw the Livermore middle school football league as a feeder straight into the NFL.

Then one day the unthinkable happened: they cancelled football.

There was something about "budgetary cuts"-this or "fiscal austerity"-that, but none of that adult nonsense meant anything to a ten-year-old who just wanted to get out on the field and play. Or, at least, none of it mattered to me. The only thing I knew for certain was that our season was cancelled, and we weren't going to be playing football any more.

That just didn't sit with me.

There were more than a few of my friends who were equally disappointed, but there was a distinct difference between them and me: I was willing to do something about it.

The natural question here would be, *What can a ten-year-old kid do about his school cancelling football?*

Most people would just assume the correct response would be *Nothing!*, but it turns out that the actual answer is *Everything!*

I made my mind up that if the school wasn't willing to be play a role in our league anymore, we were going to have our team without them.

There were more than a few of my friends who were equally disappointed, but there was a distinct difference between them and me: I was willing to do something about it.

One way or another, our team was going to have its season. No matter what.

I got my friends together and we made up our own team.

Then I put some other guys together and led them through the process of building their own roster.

Then some more guys and some more teams.

Before anyone knew what was happening I had put together a whole league.

I scheduled the games and a post-season, too.

The adults could take the funding out of the youth football program, but they couldn't keep the youth out of the football program—at least, not while I was in the mix.

To make a happy ending even sweeter, my team had a pretty good season.

At the end of the school year, the faculty gave me a special award to recognize everything I had done to keep the youth football program alive when the fiscally oriented adults had let us all down.

Some people wait for opportunities.

Smart people make them.

I cringe every time I hear someone describe a situation as being a "once in a lifetime opportunity." I rarely express my criticism out loud, but I always think to myself how foolish and self-limiting that sort of thinking is over the course of that lifetime.

They're just going to spend that lifetime waiting for opportunities to come to them?

Opportunities are not something that simply appear in your life by magic. And they're certainly not the product of waiting.

That doesn't mean that there aren't especially advantageous (and disadvantageous) situations waiting out there for you, but every opportunity is essentially a product of your own smarts, grit, and willingness to work.

If you want something to happen in your life, then don't wait for opportunities to present themselves, roll up your sleeves and get to work.

Make your own opportunities.

Do something.

CHAPTER 4
Put Your Ego in Your Pocket

Sprinkler heads spinning in the morning sun.

The shrill sound of a pea whistle.

The rhythmic *click-clack*ing of cleats walking together out to the practice field.

These are the sounds that immediately bring me back to the days of my childhood in Livermore.

And then—completely unexpectedly—those days came to a very abrupt end.

My father worked from five in the morning until seven at night. He put in his time on weekends and holidays, too. Whatever else, the man was an absolute workhorse.

And after a while, Aramark took notice. My father was promoted and transferred to become a General Manager in Southern California.

This was 1982, so there wasn't any family conference or monitored mediation about what would be "best for the children." There was just an announcement.

Then all of my stuff got packed in a box and loaded on a U-Haul. End of story.

In the middle of my eighth grade, my family made the six-hour trip down the I-5 to our new home in Irvine.

We never left California, but for the eleven-year-old me in the back of the family station wagon, we might as well have left planet Earth. I had never seen anything like Southern California before in my young life. The mansions and manicured lawns. I'd never even seen a Mercedes or BMW before this.

It was a mind-blowing—or, rather, mind expanding—experience.

I was a middle-class kid suddenly thrust into an upper-class world and it took a moment or two to get adjusted to the wealthy suburb. My parents had found a small townhouse and this afforded me access to the best schools in the area without the million-dollar price tag that came with most of the surrounding houses.

While the socio-economic environment was completely alien to me, I was relieved to find that the guys in my new school still spoke the universal language of sports.

If they were suspicious of and stand-offish toward the "new kid in town"—and, I promise you, they definitely were—all of that wore off as soon as we stepped out onto the playground. In no time, I had taken that common ground of athletics and turned it into several important friendships that I still carry with me and continue to cherish to this day.

Of course, moving to a larger and more-sophisticated area meant that the competition out on the playing field was drastically increased, as well. I was not, however, willing to let that intimidate me in any way. To the contrary, I used the challenge as all the motivation I needed to meet and exceed this new bar that had been set for me.

I knew I had to step up and so I worked every day toward achieving my football goals. I ran. And lifted. And ran drills over and over again.

When the summer was almost over, we were dead in the middle of Hell Week, back in the days when you would practice in pads, twice a day, every day, except Sunday. The practices were long and water breaks were almost nonexistent. I was battling a good friend for the starting QB position and we were both playing outside line-backer, as well.

The quarterback position brought with it a lot of extra responsibilities and I doubled-down on my commitment to work harder than I ever had before, harder than I thought I ever could.

Success was inevitable. Or so I thought.

Two weeks before the season opener, we were running a scrimmage at practice. I got caught in the human car crash that is the defensive line smashing into the offensive line.

I got popped.

Hard.

No big deal, I thought.

Even by that age, I had played so much ball that getting hit—even hit *hard*—was just a ho-hum part of my daily routine.

This time, however, there was something that felt ... *different*. This time was like nothing I'd ever felt before. I looked down at my arm and saw the bone.

There are stable fractures. (Hardly like getting hurt at all.) There are comminuted fractures, where the bones break into pieces. (Admittedly, worse.)

And then there are compound fractures, which really deserve a more menacing name that conveys the sheer devastation of an injury in which the now-jagged point of the broken bone cuts through the flesh and pokes out of the skin.

That's what happened to me.

My parents took me to the hospital and I remember sitting there, trying to resist the morbidly human temptation to sneak another peek at the bone sticking out of my arm. (I did peek. And, yes, it was every bit as disgusting as you're now imagining it to be.)

The doctor delivered a grim diagnosis to my parents. The prognosis was so serious that my father chose not to hear it at all. He shrugged off those dire words and asked the doctor, "Can't we just cast it up? How long before we can get him back out on the field?" The doctor just looked at him in disbelief ... and then scheduled my surgery.

There was no football in my freshman year of high school. No basketball, either. Or wrestling. Or baseball.

The only thing I had in my freshman year was a long, hard, and painful rehab. But I did what I had to do in order to get back on the field. I never gave into the disappointment of a missed season or succumbed to the pain of pushing towards the next season.

When my sophomore season came around, I was more than prepared to take back the quarterback slot I'd lost to injury. I was bigger and stronger than I'd ever been before. Bigger and stronger than almost everyone else on the team.

I thought my size and strength would be assets no other quarterback candidate could bring to the competition, but the coach saw something else. He called me over to the sidelines and explained that he had a new assignment for me—and it didn't include me taking snaps under center.

This was the very early 1980s and the big bodied QBs like Ben Roethlisberger and Andrew Luck had yet to prove their worth to a generation of coaches that still thought the ideal physique for the position was something between Roger Staubach-lean and Fran Tarkenton-scrawny.

So, because of the size and strength I'd worked so hard to build, the coach thought I would be better suited for some other positions— without even giving me the chance to try out for the quarterback slot.

The first new position my coach had for me was defensive line, which I was less than enthusiastic about playing. Still, as a kid who'd grown up watching The Rams' Fearsome Foursome and The Vikings' Purple People-Eaters, it was an assignment I could live with.

The second assignment, however, was on the offensive line and this held significantly less attraction for me. I had rehabbed for a year to get back under center, not climb down into the trenches and give up my body to protect someone *else* playing quarterback.

There was a painful irony in coach's decision which I think most fifteen-year-olds would've found hard to live with.

I could see how some might have even found something of a betrayal in that chain of events.

And if more than a few guys might have let those circumstances serve as a reason to quit the team outright—well, I don't know that I could really blame any of them.

The decision was devastating to me, but I was aware of three things: The first was that I had a dream of being recruited to a Division I school and then going on to play in the NFL. I wasn't about to let anything sidetrack me from pursuing my dreams with every bit of determination that I had—even a questionable coaching decision. The second was that even though I knew I was still the best quarterback on the field, I was confident that I could also become the best defensive lineman, too. And even the best offensive lineman—if that's what I had to do. The third—and most important of all—was that I wanted to play football and I knew my team needed me.

So, I put my ego in my pocket and I gave up doing what I wanted to do and I got down with doing what I knew was best for the team. My team.

21

So, I put my ego in my pocket and I gave up doing what I wanted to do and I got down with doing what I knew was best for the team. My team.

Of all the guys on that squad, I knew I had the best head for the game, the strongest arm, and the deepest reservoir of football "intangibles."

And that's why I'm not sure I could ever find the words to capture just how disappointed I was to find myself relegated to the thankless task of putting my body on the line snap-after-snap to protect the (less-qualified) kid who had "my" QB slot.

While every word of that is true, I can also say without any reservations whatsoever, that I learned as much from the experience of being shifted to the offensive and defensive lines as I have from probably any other situation in my life.

I learned the mental discipline of just grinding, play after play, not because the folks in the stands are cheering you or because the spotlight is focused on you, but just because you have a job that needs to be done and you have made the personal commitment to be the best at it.

I learned to put the interests of the organization ahead of my own personal desires, especially those that are fueled and fed by nothing more substantial that the mere whims of ego.

And I learned that sometimes in this life you get dealt setbacks, put on a path other than the one you intended to walk and, when that happens, the only thing you can do is to put your head down and keep working through.

That's exactly what I did. And I'm damn glad I did it.

CHAPTER 5
Don't Give Up

Here's a hard one. And a complicated one.

While I had been working my tail off so that I could get back out on the field and succeed in my new positions, my dad had been working just as hard at his new position as a general manager. And it had paid off. Right as my junior year was about to begin, my dad got word that the company was rewarding him with a promotion. It was a good news/bad news proposition.

The good news was the promotion itself, the well-deserved rewards for my father having worked so hard.

The bad news was that this new position required a move … to Philly.

Now, I've got absolutely nothing against The City of Brotherly Love. I love the place. But no kid wants to move in their junior year of high school, and my concerns were greater and more focused than just that general sort of adolescent opposition. I had found a spot on the team and I was legitimately afraid that moving to a new high school and starting all over, from the back of the pack—particularly, to an entirely different region of the country—would set back a college recruitment process that had already been beset by injuries.

> He worked so hard for his own success, but he was willing to give it all up to better enable me to realize my own.

Of course, complaining was about the only thing that I could do. Our house was not a democracy and my father made the decisions.

That's why I was so surprised when my dad announced that he wasn't taking the promotion he'd earned. There was no explanation offered. And none was needed.

He never said it outright, but I know that he did that for me. He worked so hard for his own success, but he was willing to give it all up to better enable me to realize my own.

And that was a side of my dad, too.

I came back for my junior year, knowing that it was maybe the most important year of all—and with the added pressure of justifying my father's sacrifice.

Everything was on the line.

And I played every down like I knew that was the case. That is, until I dislocated my left shoulder. No big deal, I just gritted my teeth and they just popped it back in. I went back out on the field and played until my shoulder popped back out.

Grit teeth. Pop shoulder. Repeat.

We continued this game of me as a human action figure until the shoulder got so bad that they simply couldn't pop it back in anymore. Or, at least, there was nothing left to hold my shoulder in place.

My junior year we had a terrible season, our team was definitely not making the playoffs, but even with my dislocated shoulder and a perfectly good reason to hang it up for the year to go get the surgery I badly needed, I still refused to miss even a single game.

It was football and I loved to play the game, hurt or not hurt.

The season ended and I finally had surgery that my shoulder had needed for months.

The off-season was rehab and reconditioning, but it was all familiar ground to me by now.

I returned for my senior year knowing that there were some very serious eyes on me, knowing that I wasn't the only one who had made some significant sacrifices for the chance for me to demonstrate to college scouts what I could do on a football field.

The first snap of that first game, I exploded off of the line like the freak force of nature I was. I closed my eyes and could picture our mailbox stuffed with thick envelopes from every Division I program in the country.

The second play of that game—the second play of my senior year—I felt a very specific pain that I had become accustomed to and knew immediately that I'd separated my shoulder.

The right one this time.

There was no time for the now all-too-familiar pattern of triage-rehab-return. It was my senior year and I knew that everything was on the line, it was now or never.

I decided to play through the excruciating pain and the resulting limitations that my condition caused me on the field. Our team was having a good year and we had a shot to make the playoffs. I wasn't about to miss that opportunity or let my team (or my dad) down by not playing. I wasn't about to let a little thing like my shoulder popping out of the socket every game hold me back.

Since there wasn't an opportunity for the surgery and rehab I needed, the trainers turned to what they thought was the next best solution: tape. Not quite duct tape, but the philosophy was basically the same.

Before every game, the trainers would do their best to construct a spider-web of kinesio tape that would offer the joint a modicum of support that my own ligaments could not. This process essentially entailed taping most of my right arm to my body.

This might have been an effective fix if I had been on the debate team, but I was assigned to play the offensive and defensive lines on a team that was competitive on a county level and that played an incredibly tough schedule that more than justified that ranking.

No matter which side of the ball I was lined up on, I found myself matched up against some guy who was every bit as big as I was and (almost) as mean. My only disadvantage was that he had the use of *both* of his arms.

So, losing the full use of my right arm became something of an, well, on-field *issue*.

Imagine for a moment, being on the offensive line with a wall of guys (6'3" or bigger, all of them over 250 lbs.) and you have to hold them back with one hand literally tied behind your back—or, at least, taped to your side.

Now, get up off the ground, dust yourself off, and do it all again from the defensive side.

And repeat. Again and again. For the full sixty minutes.

This was my senior season.

I got banged up. A lot. O-lines ganged up on me. D-lines swarmed me.

When the tape failed and my shoulder popped out of its socket, the trainers would pop it back in and put me back out on the field. If it popped out again, they'd just pop it back again.

Although I never stopped fighting—and I'm proud to say I more than held my own for a one-armed man—the injury was too much for me to put on the sort of season-long demonstration I knew I was capable of, the kind of show that would have drawn the scholarship offers from those Division I programs I had wanted to be a part of since the very first time I had ever put on pads.

The collegiate interest in me cooled.

Despite all my dedication, hard work and—if I'm choosing honesty over modesty—all of my God-given talent, no one was interested.

All this, despite that fact that I was playing through injuries that would have ended almost anyone else's season—and career. Despite the many sacrifices. The two-a-days in the summer heat. The excruciating rehabs. The focus on playbooks (sometimes to the exclusion of schoolbook.). Despite everything, I could no longer deny that my dream had eluded me … for the time being.

But that was all just a temporary delay. Not an end of the dream, just a return to trenches to work for another chance to make it all come true.

I was willing to make the necessary concession that came in accepting that my plans of playing for a major Division I football powerhouse had been derailed, but I refused to accept that these results were final or to surrender my fate to any other force beyond my own determination. I would not relinquish my power to shape the life I was intent on living.

There are any number of take-aways I hope to share with you, but I don't think there are any more important than this: Failure will be a part of your life. So will adversity. I don't care what your goal is, whether that's on the playing field or in the board room. If your goal is big enough to sustain you for a lifetime, then there will certainly be times when you fall short. It's unavoidable.

And that's not a bad thing. The important thing is that you learn from those experiences, that you allow the fire of failure to galvanize you and make you more resistant to the uncontrollable forces of this life.

Don't blame others or cry about your circumstances. Just refocus on what you need to do, revise your plan accordingly, and then get back to work.

But don't ever give up.

This is a hard life, I know, but the opportunities it offers are limited only by your faith in yourself, your dedication to your dreams, and your commitment to work harder than anyone else to achieve them.

CHAPTER 6
Be Kind

That was my high school football career.

Sacrifice and dedication. Surgery and rehabilitation.

The same routine. Over and over.

At the time, I was (understandably, I hope) focused on my teen-aged self.

My dreams of playing Division I and then professional football.

My injuries.

My surgery and rehab.

I understand why I saw it that way, but I regret that I did.

Looking back on that time now—particularly since I'm now a dad and having kids of my own has allowed me to view my past through a more mature lens of parenthood—I can't imagine what the experience must have been like for my mother.

The sad fact of life is that no matter how painful it is out there on the field, every hit a kid takes in the game hurts the parents even more. Knowing that now, I can't fathom what it must have been like for my mom to sit in the stands every Friday and see her oldest boy go through the sort of physical pain I went through from kick-off to final whistle.

Every game. Week after week.

I'm amazed now that she never once complained or tried to talk me out of my mad pursuit. It would have been an easy out for her, but she never once took advantage of it—even knowing that I would've done anything for her. Instead, she bore a mother's pain with her big, bright smile, all too aware that she couldn't say a thing about her ordeal without killing my dream.

She just smiled.

And she was the one who came to my room when the doctor's prognosis was grim or the physical therapy didn't seem like it was working fast enough and told me, "It's all right to question your dreams from time to time, but don't you ever give up on yourself. Because if there's one thing I'm sure of in all my heart, it's that one day you're going to make all of your dreams come true."

That was my mom.

And she wasn't that way just to me. She was the "house mom" of the neighborhood, of my team, of my friends. Every weekend she always had the door open and there were always guys from the team staying for dinner or friends sleeping over.

My teenage self never gave it a thought at the time except that this was the sort of thing that moms did. I can see now, however, that her "open house" policy was a subtle and completely successful covert operation to keep me and my friends out of trouble and away from the temptations that were all too abundant and all around us.

My dad had the military background. He was the coach who always demanded more.

My mom was just the opposite. She wasn't stingy with the hugs, and when she knew I needed one, she gave me two. With her quiet, but constant support she did more to foster my belief in myself than anyone else in my life.

And when I look back on it now, I think, she was probably the toughest Jones of us all.

There have always been great demands put on me and, as a result, I'm not hesitant about putting expectations on anyone else, nor am I slow in reverting to that coach mentality of putting boot to ass, if that's what need to get things done.

At the same time, however, my mother unintentionally taught me one of the greatest lessons in business management with her kindness and compassion. I admit that I'm quick to bark orders and demand from others the same level of performance that I expect from myself, but I'm equally quick to nurture my team and to offer support to those who need it.

My mom gave me that balance. She made me a better manager. A better man, too.

Toughness is necessary.

But sometimes it's best to try a little tenderness. And always be kind.

CHAPTER 7
Mentor

There's no question that football was the most important thing to me in my high school years, but it was not the only thing that captured my interest.

It would be somewhat misleading to say that I was enraptured by the lavish homes and exotic cars that were an everyday part of my classmate's lives. The truth of the matter is that the purely material trappings of wealth or what is often perceived as success have never held any particular allure for me. That's not to say that I cannot appreciate some of the finer things in life, only that they have never offered me the substantial motivation they seem to ignite in some others. I simply could never have worked as hard as I have every day of my life if the only payout at the end of the long, hard road had been nothing but a collection of things.

No, I have never done anything simply for the money. At least, not *just* for the money. Instead, I was mesmerized by the intangible aura of the successful men that I met as the new kid in Irvine, California. The way they conducted themselves. Their confidence.

I think somehow, I recognized that there was another game besides football. One just as tough (in its way) and every bit as demanding in the level of sacrifice and commitment it required to come out on top. That game was business and, as far as I was concerned, these gentlemen—the fathers of my friends and girlfriends—were every bit the superstars as any NFL quarterback or wide receiver.

For that reason, I will freely confess that there was more than one Saturday night when I arrived at a girl's house to pick her up for a date, went through the traditionally awkward ritual of meeting her father and then, rather than going out to the movies or whatever our plans were supposed to be, spent the evening happily talking to her father about his business and picking his brain.

(Of course, when I say "happily," I mean for me, not her. For some reason, my dates were never thrilled to spend the evening with me talking business with their dads.)

In this way, I suppose I had many mentors during those all-important years of development. One, however, was particularly important to me throughout my life and I can honestly say that there's good reason to believe that I never could have become the man I am today if it hadn't been for his unwavering support and his spot-on guidance.

When I met Dave Roberson, he was just my friend's dad. In a short period of time, however, he became like a father to me, as well. That's no slam on my own father. There was no sense of replacing one for the other, but rather just further supplementing the corps of men who were helping to shepherd me through adolescence.

In the same spirit as Richard Kiyosaki's best-seller *Rich Dad, Poor Dad*, I saw my own father as my "Hard Working Dad" and Mr. Roberson as my "Smart Working Dad."

While so many of the adults whom I encountered tended to regard me as just another teen or were inclined to interact with me solely on the basis of my role on the football team, Mr. Roberson seemed to take an almost immediate interest in me as the man he seemed confident I could become. From that first meeting, he was intent on grooming me to be prepared for taking on that future. For Mr. Roberson, this included always making sure that I always had enough cash in my pocket to hold my own with the other kids whose allowances and trust funds kept them consistently well funded. Somehow, he understood that while my father had a good job and was an excellent provider, there wasn't a household income there that could give me the free-spending cash that all of my other peers took for granted.

So, without ever saying a word to me or making it look to anyone (most important of all, my own father) that there was any consideration of anything even remotely bordering on charity, Mr. Roberson always had a series of odd jobs that he was eager to (over)pay me for doing. Running errands. Driving him and his clients around town. Whatever he needed to be done, I was glad to do.

And while I was certainly appreciative of the compensation that came in the form of the thick fold of bills that he would casually press into my hand, I was even more grateful for the opportunity to be around him and learn through observation.

Mr. Roberson had made his fortune in insurance and I learned more from simply driving him around Orange County and listening to him handle his business than I ever did getting my MBA (and I learned *a lot* from my MBA program.)

He exuded class and an easy confidence that I immediately made designs to emulate and which I have since tried to carry with me into every interaction I have. More than anything, Mr. Roberson taught me the importance of a mentor; not only the advantage of having others to offer experienced guidance and counseling, but also the benefits to be gained on the other side of that equation, in offering advice to and taking care of others.

With Mr. Roberson very much in mind, I have tried to incorporate his kind nature and anonymous acts of altruism into my management style. While I have always been keenly focused on the success of my company, I have been equally committed to pushing every employee I have ever had to realize their true potential as individuals. And the rewards for this have been tremendous—for all involved.

I will tell you that, at the end of the day, there is absolutely no question in my mind that what a leader gets out of their team members is directly related to the investment that he is willing to make *in* them.

At the end of the day, there is absolutely no question in my mind but that what a leader gets out of their team members is directly related to the investment that he is willing to make in them.

Most of all, I was forever changed by Mr. Roberson's kindness. I know that if he had ever been confronted by his good deeds, he surely would have dismissed his altruism as a simple thing. He *needed* his car washed or a ride to the airport, that's all.

The truth of the matter, however, is much larger than that.

This man's care and compassion changed my life and I have always tried to honor him by paying that kindness forward. To this day, I go out of my way to identify those individuals who I think might benefit from the same sort of extra attention and interaction that Mr. Roberson—and a host of other mentors—have invested in me over the years.

I am quick to offer my advice or assistance and, where needed, the same sort of ready pocket-money that Mr. Roberson gave me.

Again, I follow this course of action not simply for the advantages that I can convey on others, but also for the immeasurable rewards that these acts bring back to me—often in the most unexpected ways.

Be kind. It's just that simple. Not just because it's the right thing to do, but because it makes good business sense.

CHAPTER 8
No Excuses (Or Complaints)

The spring of my senior year in high school passed without the college commitment ceremony I'd been preparing for ever since I'd organized my school league back in elementary school.

There was no press conference, no teasing selection of hats spread out on a table during a signing ceremony in the high school gym. There was no dramatic moment of pause while everyone in the gymnasium waited breathlessly to see where I'd be playing football in the fall.

Alabama, like his dad?

Did a national title have him looking to Oklahoma?

Or was he staying closer to home, maybe UCLA? USC?

There was none of that.

Instead, there was another surgery, this time to repair the separated right shoulder that no trainer on earth could have taped back into place any longer. Another excruciating round of rehab. The (now all-too-familiar) Road to Recovery.

And there was all the time in the world to consider a "next step" that I never could have envisioned I'd be forced to face.

I suppose I could have gone to a smaller school. Division II or III. I could have played football on what then would've been to me then an almost-recreational level and focused on getting an education. I could have, but ...

I was not willing to give up on my dream of playing professional football. So, I decided that I would head off to a junior college, play my tail off (as I always did), and then earn a spot on a Division I team as a transfer.

Was it a perfect plan? Absolutely not. But it was mine. And I was certain that I could make it work. All of it.

Over time, I have learned that this is a vital component of realizing any meaningful sort of success. As the poet Robert Burns wrote, "*The best laid schemes o' mice an' men, gang aft a-gley.*"

That means things don't always work out. At least, not the way you thought they would. Or hoped they would. That is not, however, a reason to give up—as far too many people readily do. Instead, those "altered" plans only offer us a reason to try even harder.

That's what I did.

I chose Saddleback Junior College in Mission Viejo, California, as the place from which to make my Phoenix-like ascension back to Division I consideration and from there straight into the NFL.

I showed up for training camp at Saddleback that summer … and dislocated my surgically repaired right shoulder. Again. This time the injury cost me a whole year of rehab.

But when that year was done, I returned to Saddleback ready to hit the ground running. In fact, I hit everything. Hard. (Even for me.)

The coach had pulled me from the offensive line and that allowed me to concentrate on playing defense, switching between defensive end and outside linebacker, both of which I excelled at. It also gave me an opportunity to catch my breath during the game (something I couldn't do when I played both ways), and so every time I took the field I was fresh and ready to go.

I had a great season. A beast of a season. In fact, almost everyone on the squad had a great season.

Before we knew it, my Gauchos—(yes, we were the Saddleback Gauchos)—were playing in the NJCAA Championship game for the national title. Unfortunately, we didn't walk away with the championship that year, but the big game was still a significant stage and it provided me an opportunity to capture the attention of a number of Division I schools who had sent representatives to scout a showcase of the best junior college talent.

I was among those who caught some of that national spotlight. TCU. Kansas State. UNLV.

I'd finally realized the goal I'd long ago set for myself by garnering multiple Division I offers. Somehow, however, in that long-dreamt-of moment, the achievement still wasn't enough to satisfy me. The numerous offers that had come to me after my first year were all perfectly respectable, but some of my teammates who'd spent two years with the Gauchos were now going to schools like Georgia, Tennessee, and Stanford. The Promised Land. Football factories.

Keep in mind, my goal at the time wasn't to get into a Division I university for the sake of gaining an education, college was just a stop on the way. A very necessary stepping stone.

The dream was the pros. The NFL.

So, with that singular goal in mind, I decided to put all my chips on the line and rather than taking any of those "lesser" Division I offers, I returned to Saddleback for another roll of the dice. What I hadn't factored into my considerations and eventual decision was that with so many of my second-year teammates having moved on to those same big name schools that I wanted to attend, the squad that actually returned to Saddleback for my second year was significantly depleted and comprised mainly of new guys. Because of this, the collective talent pool was nowhere near as deep as it had been during my first year and the team never gelled personally the way that we had in our run for the national title.

That season was a significant disappointment. There was no return to the NJCAA Championship for the Gauchos in my second year. To make matters worse, the talent-drain meant that the coach felt it necessary to put me back on the offensive line, something I had wanted to avoid ever since I'd gotten that assignment as a high school sophomore.

People want results, not excuses.

I was still playing defense, too. Outside linebacker. Oh, and special teams, too. So, I was literally on the field for every play of the game. Every second of those sixty minutes.

The physical demands of those assignments were brutal.

I remember one game in particular. It was a typical autumn afternoon in Mission Viejo, which meant it was like 110 degrees, high sun, and a strong Santa Ana blowing. We were playing Mount San Antonio College and they featured a running back named Leonard Russell. The guy was a beast at 6'2", 240 lbs.

A couple years later, he would go in the first round of the 1991 NFL Draft to the New England Patriots and would then run straight through pro defense after pro defense until he was named Offensive Rookie of the Year.

On that day, however, he ran straight into me. Over and over again. I'd no sooner get done with my defensive duties of trying to contain Leonard, then I was out on special teams. And then right back out on the offensive line. Then special teams. And then back to trying to stop the unstoppable Leonard Russell.

At the end of the first quarter, I was tired. During the half, I was exhausted. And by the time the clock had run on the third quarter, I was more like the walking dead ... with a full quarter still left to play.

Somewhere on that dizzying day, I missed a tackle on Russell. (Just like most of the NFL would do over the course of his six-year pro career.) My coach was furious. He hollered at me to come to him at the sidelines, grabbed my face mask, and proceeded to chew me out for having let Russell get past me.

I was beyond exhausted. Dehydrated and completed depleted. My head spun. The ground beneath me spun, too. And then I vomited. All over the coach's shoes.

When I was done retching, I just turned right around and went back out to my position as outside linebacker and doubled-down on my efforts to stop Russell.

What I didn't do was complain or offer excuses. The fact of the matter was that I *had* missed the tackle. There were reasons for it— excellent reasons and plenty of them—but I never offered one of them. Not to the coach. My teammates. Or myself.

They may have been excellent reasons, but not one of them mattered. The end result was the same. I had given up yards. End of story. Period.

In this world you're going to face difficulties. Everyone does. And that's why no one is particularly interested in yours. Each of us already has plenty of our own.

Still, there are far too many people who have nothing to offer but explanations or complaints. Whether it's in football or business or any other aspect of your life, the bitching and the finger pointing won't serve any practical purpose, they won't get you where you need to go. If your assignment is to stop Leonard Russell, then find a way to stop him. If you come up short, try harder next time. Get it done. But keep your mouth shut.

People want results, not excuses. And they will naturally gravitate toward those who get things done and away from those who are awash in a sea of self-pitying negativity.

At the end of that season, there was a team banquet and the coach got up to address all of those assembled. He brought up the shoe-barf incident and laughed, remarking that in the thirty-five years he'd been coaching football no other player had ever thrown up on his shoes. Not once.

In the end, it didn't matter that we had ultimately lost that game. Or that I had ruined a perfectly good pair of shoes for the coach. If anything, that unfortunate event had only cemented his respect for me because it was an unpleasant testament to the fact that I would play right up until my body gave out—and then continue beyond. It was evidence that while some vile things might come out of my mouth, complaints and excuses were not among them.

CHAPTER 9
Stand on Your Own

After a disappointing second season at Saddleback, in which my responsibilities on both sides of the ball had physically limited my ability to put on the kind of showcase that would attract the big Division I schools I was looking for, there were no suitors from University of Alabama or Stanford or any of the big-name programs I'd been dreaming about my entire life.

Only Oregon State came knocking at my door. They offered me a sweet deal, a full ride. I was less than excited, however, because the Beavers had gone 1–10 the year before and I didn't see the sense in becoming a part of a losing program that wasn't going to guarantee me the attention of NFL scouts.

It wasn't, however, just the Beavers and their losing ways that shaped my outlook. At that time in my life, there was a much more attractive figure in the equation. *Much* more attractive.

During my second year at Saddleback, I started dating a cheerleader. She was great. We were great. And I was happy with everything until one night she announced that there was a problem with our relationship: distance. She was transferring to California Polytechnic State University in San Luis Obispo.

I, however, didn't see the difficulty in that, not at all. While the only Division I interest had come from Oregon State, I was a hotly pursued prospect with a good number of Division II schools. As it happened, Cal Poly had been among the crowd of those Division II suitors and when I worked out for their football coach that interest turned to pure love.

So, it seemed to the twenty-year-old-me like a perfect decision all-the-way-around. If I wasn't going to be able to move on to the Division I school of my choice, then I could simply take the offer to become a Cal Poly Mustang and keep the love alive. Mine for that cheerleader. And Cal Poly's coach's for me.

Looking back at it now, I can see all of the flaws in my decision-making process, but I was happy enough with it at the time. Of course, I knew Cal Poly wasn't a football factory. And while enthusiastic, I don't think I'd ever confused that personal situation into thinking that the cheerleader and I were soulmates or that what was happening between us was a lifelong sort of thing.

But I did care about her. And in my young life, which had been characterized by so much physical pain, a little bit of comfort was more important to me than I think anyone ever could have understood. Or, at least, more important than my father realized.

For the entirety of my life, my father had been more of a coach than a dad. He yelled more than he talked, and he talked more than he listened. That's not to say that I didn't always understand that his motivation for all of this was his love for me or that all he really wanted for me was to make the most of my opportunities—opportunities that maybe he felt he'd let slip through his own fingers. I knew that then. (And I still do.) But even with that consolation, when I remember my father, those memories most often come back to me at *full* volume.

So, when I proudly announced to my family that I'd be attending Cal Poly in the coming fall, I was taken aback when my father fell uncharacteristically silent. I (mis)took it as a good sign.

A little while later that day, he surprised me by suddenly appearing at my bedroom door and calmly asking, "Do you know what you are?"

"What?"

He didn't yell as he usually did. He just looked at me and said, "You're pussy-whipped." I was shocked. Or, at least, I didn't say anything back. He stood there for a moment, silent himself, and then said what was really on his mind, but the words were even quieter still. "I have never been so disappointed in you in my life."

Then, without another word, he was gone.

It's funny, but what struck me first was a sort childish amazement (and admiration) that my father actually *knew* that word. I had no idea my dad had been that "cool."

What hit me next wasn't necessarily the words he'd chosen—although, they were certainly hurtful in their own right. What stung the most was just how quiet he had been when he'd said them, like after a lifetime of screaming at me to push myself harder, he no longer saw the worth in wasting that level of effort on me.

What stung the most was just how quiet he had been when he'd said them, like after a lifetime of screaming at me to push myself harder, he no longer saw the worth in wasting that level of effort on me.

It was that quiet that hurt me the most. Crushed me.

I suppose most boys find a hero in their father and I certainly found one in mine. But there was more to our relationship than just that easy role play. I was born into a line of men who were determined to make their sons "better" than themselves, to drive them to level of success that life had somehow unfairly robbed from them. My father was not only my hero, he was the bar that he was determined I had to get over.

Sitting there on my bed in that terrible quiet, what I felt more than anything else was I was alone. Terribly alone. Maybe for the first time ever. And that was a watershed moment for me.

Here's the thing. People are going to disagree with you from time to time. Sometimes those conflicts will be minor and sometimes they will rip relationships apart. Doesn't matter. That can't change anything—at least, not about your dream.

Your dream is yours. And yours alone.

And sometimes that means standing up for you and your dream when absolutely no one else will. My dad's words hit harder than any running back charging through the hole, but I did what I did every time I had such a ferocious collision on the field … I got up. I didn't sit on that bed for long. I didn't wallow in my father's words.

I resolved to use them as I had always used every disappointment, setback, and cheap shot I've been given: as fuel to motivate myself to keep moving forward, faster and more forcefully than ever.

And then, when I thought I had finally come to terms with it all, something else hit me. Hit me so much harder than my dad's words. I was struck by a fact: he was right. Absolutely, 110 percent right.

He hadn't meant what he'd said as a verbal assault, he'd merely been calling me out on my own bullshit. There it was.

I *had* been pussy-whipped. And even worse, I had lied to myself. I had allowed all sort of nonsense to interfere with the singularity of my vision.

I'd started that afternoon resenting my father, but the evening found me only being more grateful than ever. He had exercised restraint on his own emotions to say to me what I should've said to myself.

Honesty is a necessity in this life. But complete truthfulness is most essential of all in your relationship with yourself. Once you begin to deceive yourself to fulfill some lesser, temporary desire, the entirety of your life plan falls into jeopardy.

I remind myself of that incident often.

I'm not one to concern myself with regrets or what-could've-beens. So, I'm not interested in pursuing those pointless considerations of what might have happened if I'd taken the spot in Oregon State. I do, however, replay those events for the purpose of keeping myself completely honest with me. I see my old man standing in that bedroom doorway and I remind myself not to bullshit myself. Not ever.

CHAPTER 10
Adapt

The factor that I had never really considered about Cal Poly was that it was an excellent school. A *really* excellent school. And for the first time in my life that comment wasn't an evaluation of their football program.

Cal Poly was a serious academic institution attended by twenty thousand (give or take) young adults, the vast majority of whom were laser-focused on their studies and a future beyond the classroom. And suddenly I was one of them.

I have to admit that the prospect ahead of me, the challenge of rising to their collective academic expectations, seemed daunting at first. In fact, by the time I was heading off for the start of that school year, the entire prospect was significantly less inviting than I had found it just a few weeks earlier.

The cheerleader and I had broken-up. (No surprise there.) And there was absolutely no safety net for me any longer. My spot on the roster at Oregon State, along with the scholarship that went with it, had been passed along to someone else when I'd told the coach I wasn't interested in attending. (Yes, I had a made an "On second-thought …" call to the coach there.)

If I didn't make it at Cal Poly, there was no longer anywhere else to go.

Don't get me wrong. I was a smart kid and had always gotten good grades (decent, anyway), but the bookwork had always taken a backseat to the playbook. Now, all of a sudden—and almost unexpectedly—I found myself at a university where academics were far more important than athletics and that was an entirely new environment for me, one which brought with it a completely different paradigm.

I was so far out of my element that I turned out for registration and class selection without any independent idea about what courses I should take or what major I should pursue. Not knowing exactly what to do, I called up my father and asked what he thought I should do.

He didn't hesitate. "Well, you want to coach football, so it seems the natural thing to do would be to take physical education." Just that simple. My future was a done deal to him and he saw it continuing to revolve around football.

I understood. But I wasn't nearly as certain as he'd been. I'd spent my entire life up until that one pivotal moment in the registrar's office absolutely convinced that I was going to be a professional football player. I had never considered any other possibility or let doubt linger long enough at the back of my thoughts that I ever saw more than a glimpse of me doing anything else.

While I was certainly as hot as ever on pursuing that goal, I have to admit that there was a nagging reality check whispering at the back of my brain. *What if it all doesn't work out exactly the way that you want it to?*

In my new surroundings at Cal Poly, however, the prospect of some other previously unconsidered career didn't seem to me so much like a failure as it did a simple necessity. Or luxury. In fact, the more I thought about it and the more exciting those unexplored possibilities became to me, I found that the only lingering doubt I had in my mind was whether I really wanted to spend that bright, new future as a football coach.

The call to my father hadn't settled anything. In fact, it had only opened up a thousand new questions. Needing some greater sense of direction, I called my mentor, Dave Roberson, and asked him what he thought I should do.

He didn't hesitate either. "I was a political science major and I think that would be a good fit for you. Whatever you want to do afterward—law school, business, whatever—you'll be able to put your poly sci degree to work."

It was an important moment. In a way, the doors of the world came open. My father had laid out one path to a very definite future and I understood that, but my mentor had sketched out another, more promising possibility.

Sports had always come easily to me. There had never been any real struggle for me there. Intellectually, I had always understood what I was supposed to do, and physically I had always possessed the skills necessary to get that done.

I considered them both and I saw both versions of my life, but in the end only one seemed like *my* life. I went with the Smart-Working Dad, over my Hard-Working Dad. I entered Cal Poly as a political science major.

Of course, declaring the major was the easiest part of getting the degree. Up to this point, I had never really applied the same merciless and methodical work process that I brought to football to my studies. Cal Poly demanded that I change that.

Despite the commitment and sacrifice that athletics had always demanded of me, sports had always come easily to me. There had never been any real struggle for me there. Intellectually, I had always understood what I was supposed to do, and physically I had always possessed the skills necessary to get that done.

Academics was something completely different.

At the same time, however, I soon discovered that applying those same fundamental principles I'd learned on the practice and playing fields to my work in the classroom produced very similar success. It was simple. Show up prepared. Never accept less than your maximum effort. Be the hardest worker.

Whatever the task may be, keep doing that until it becomes second nature. And then do it some more.

CHAPTER 11
Accept the Facts

Of course, going to Cal Poly wasn't merely a transition from student–athlete to serious student. In addition to those increased emphasis on academics, my responsibilities to the football program remained the same (and with them my own personal commitment to make it to the NFL). It was a step up, moving from a junior college program to Division II.

And so, I studied textbooks *and* playbooks. I went to practice and then to class and then right back to practice.

In no time (or, at least, that's how it seems looking back on it now), I was enjoying the same sort of success in my studies that I'd always found on the playing field. That was a good thing, too.

My first year at Cal Poly was essentially my junior year of college and so I took the field that season knowing how important those eleven games were to the fulfillment of the pro dream I'd worked so hard to make a reality. Just eleven games to make the plays that would earn me some measure of national recognition. Eleven opportunities to show the football world what I could do. Eleven chances to put everything I had on the line and roll the dice.

Make it or break it. Go big or go home.

My defensive coordinator at Cal Poly was a legend in football. He had coached at all of the major Division I programs. He'd had stints in the USFL and NFL. He was just a certified badass who demanded that you go through as much pain and agony as you needed to in order to execute on your assignments out on the field.

He would not settle for less than your full intensity every minute of every game, every practice. Everything you did for him required your total commitment.

August was a brutal training camp that included three practices a day. Full pads and full contact hitting all three practices. No rest and damn few water breaks. The experience was exhausting.

Practice would start at 6:00 a.m. with workouts. Breakfast, which you had to force yourself to eat. Practice in pads. Lunch, which you had to be careful not to force yourself to eat too much or you would get sick because you were already so hot and thirsty. Study in the film room. Back out on the broiling hot field for afternoon practice in pads. Films. Dinner. Evening practice for those of us on special teams. Films. Repeat.

Every day. All day. For the entire month of August.

When September came along, we were ready to get out on the field and play, but we were even more relieved that there was something else to break up the brutal routine of practice.

The first game of the season I was lined up as defensive end. The tight end blocked down and all of a sudden, I saw a three-hundred-pound lineman charging right at me.

No problem. I was 6'2" and 240 pounds of muscle and hard-hitting bad attitude. I had made a career out of rolling over lineman bigger than him and I wasn't about to back away from this guy. I charged at him with everything I had, knowing that he was three steps away from me knocking him on his ass. Three. Two. One.

Our bodies collided like two trucks at an intersection. That human explosion was something I had simply made a part of my life. This time, however, something was different.

This time I heard a loud *crack* in my neck and both my arms immediately fell limp. My neck seemed frozen and I was unable to turn my head at all.

Somehow I managed to pull myself up off of the field and moved off to the sidelines under my own power.

My coach stopped me before I could take a seat on the bench. "Get your ass back out in that huddle."

I said, "But Coach, I think I just broke my neck. I can't feel my arms. I can't move my head."

My coach was not concerned. "Get your ass back out on that field!"

I did what I had been told to do and jogged back out onto the field, but what took only a few steps and a couple of seconds seemed like forever. And there was plenty of time to think about lots of things—things that hadn't crossed my mind before.

Obviously, I was worried that I might have just broken my neck and what that might mean down the road for me. I was angry (maybe even a little hurt and betrayed) that my coach wasn't interested in anything besides getting me back out onto the field. But most of all, I remember that moment as the first time in my life that I had ever thought to myself that I didn't want to play football. Not anymore.

For the next series of plays, I lined up without being able to feel or move my arms and my field of vision was restricted to staring straight ahead. I was a sitting duck. They ran three plays and by some miracle, none of them came anywhere near me. If they had called a rushing play through my zone, I don't know what a guy with (essentially) no arms could've done—except get hurt even worse.

They punted and the defense came off of the field.

I went over to the trainer and told him, "I think I just broke my neck."

He had evidently been trained in bedside manner by the coach. "It's probably just a stinger. Go out there, you'll be fine."

I finished the game somehow, but even today I can't explain how I managed to do what I did with two arms that weren't working right and a neck that wouldn't move.

Severely injuring my neck didn't end my season—although I'm certain that under modern medical protocols it certainly would have put a stop to it if I had been playing today. From this point on in the season, I had a daily ritual to ice both my shoulders, both my knees, and my neck. I would lay on bags of ice until the pain subsided or I just lapsed into exhaustion. I would wake up in puddles of melted ice and trudge off to the shower, walking like a ninety-year-old man.

Week after week, I carried on this protocol, but my neck never got any better. I was afraid to go to the doctor because that would certainly mean I would miss practice and probably a good deal of playing time, too.

And if I'm completely honest, I think I was so frightened of hearing the diagnosis "broken neck"—the tragedies of Daryl Stingley, Mike Utleym and Dennis Byrd loomed large—that I was more comfortable living with the constant excruciating pain than I would have been with coming to terms with those limitations.

Still, I was determined to play and this required not only dealing with the excruciating pain, but also struggling through the inescapable physical restrictions that the collective injuries placed on my on-field performance. That's no excuse, just truth. With my neck (and the other injuries I'd endured along the way), I just wasn't able to be the player that I wanted to be—or that I knew in my heart I could be if I were just given the chance to take the field reasonably healthy.

That doesn't mean, however, that I didn't play my heart out every single down—despite those limitations. I did.

In the end, our Mustangs went deep into the Division II playoffs. Eventually, we wound up losing to North Dakota State, a perennial power in Division II and Division I AA football for decades. That year, the Bison ultimately claimed the championship title, so there was no shame in having ended our season with them.

However, at the end of this particular season, I knew it would be my last.

I had never worried about playing hurt before in my life. In fact, if anything, I always regarded my willingness to put my personal welfare aside for the good of the team and endure whatever suffering came my way as a demonstration of my limitless commitment to my team and my teammates. And, maybe just maybe, a sign of my personal strength and character, too.

This time it was different. I had gone through the entire season without being able to move my neck and the situation hadn't gotten any better with time. I was seriously concerned that I was just a bad hit (or even a simple twist of the neck) away from a lifetime of being paralyzed or somehow seriously incapacitated and limited in my movements for the rest of my life.

But it wasn't the neck that hurt most of all. In my entire football career, I had always been surrounded by tough coaches who wanted to win and demanded that I make the physical sacrifices necessary to put that win on the board—I'd certainly put my own father in their group. But never before had I played for a coach who didn't give a damn about his players or their health and welfare. My other coaches were tough, but they were always making sure you were all right as a player, and your health was their ultimate concern. Win or lose, they were all focused, first and foremost, on you just being able to walk off of the field.

It was a different time and I am a big proponent of the multiple changes that have been enacted in the rules of the game and team protocols to protect student-athletes. Moreover, as a strong supporter of Mustang football—(I'm proud to say that the locker room that was once a second home to me now bears my name as a benefactor of the program that did so much for me)—I am grateful that Cal Poly has been at the forefront of this commitment to make the game I love as safe as possible for the young men who play it.

But, as I've said, this was a different day and I felt that this particular individual was more focused on the wins and losses than the welfare of his players.

With the advantage of the passage of time and now viewing the situation through a more mature lens, I'm not prepared to pass any sort of judgment. I can only say that prior to this experience, football had always been a covenant relationship for me.

Sure, I had my own personal ambitions within the game, but I played my heart out for the fans, I bled for my teammates, and I gave everything that I had (body and soul) for my coaches just like they were my very own father.

And every time I took the field, I always felt the return on all of those relationships.

In this particular situation, however, there was no give-and-take. There wasn't the sort of mutual concern and respect that I had always experienced with my other coaches throughout my football career. That realization was soul crushing to me.

For the first time in my career, I didn't feel like I was playing football as part of a team. Without that element of camaraderie, I began to question my reason for continuing. (And that is why, to this day, I take every step possible to let all of my employees/teammates know that I appreciate and support them 110 percent, and most importantly, I will never ask them to do anything I will not personally do myself.)

And it wasn't just that single injury—although you'd think that a serious neck injury alone would be sufficient to drive me to certain conclusions about my career.

The combination of injuries was getting the better of me, to the point that I could barely walk, let alone run.

By this time, I had been playing football at a highly competitive level for more than ten years. There were more surgeries than I could count and more rehabs than I wanted to remember. That nearly-broken neck only heightened the limitations put on me by my already-surgically-repaired shoulders. My back ached. My knees clicked.

My body was just broken.

I had demanded what most people never ask of their bodies—and then I had pushed myself harder still.

When my body wanted to rest, I had practiced and trained

When my body wanted to heal, I had played hurt.

I had accomplished everything in my athletic career through sheer force of will, but now there was nothing left *but* will.

That was all I had left.

My desire still burned every bit as white-hot, but I could no longer avoid the inescapable fact that there simply wasn't anything more that I could do physically to perform at the exceptional standards necessary to make it to the professional level of football at which I had always dreamed of playing.

That was it.

No doubt.

No question.

The dream was over. Period.

The end of the line was hard to face. But it wasn't just as simple as making a personal decision and walking away. There was also a financial decision at stake here, too.

I had gone to Cal Poly on a full football scholarship, so tuition, room and board, books, and all of my expenses had been covered by the school. If I walked away from football, it meant giving up all of that. And I wasn't sure who was going to pick up the tab without that scholarship.

I knew better than to raise the issue with my dad, so I drove home one weekend to talk to my mom. And, just like always, she was there for me in a remarkable way. She told me that I had already done so much with football, but maybe I had reached a point in my life where my dream had to change to include something else instead.

Much of what I have to say within these pages is based on the simple premises of finding a dream, stoking the fires of ambition, and then pursuing those goals with absolutely everything that you have—and then finding a little more and trying even harder.

I brought up the financial issue and she just smiled. She assured me that whatever costs our family had to incur, they would do what they had always done and pay them. A son who was unhappy, much less paralyzed or seriously hurt, wasn't worth all of the money in the world to her.

Sometimes, even when you know what the answer is, you just need to hear someone else say those words out loud and my mom was the best at telling me the truth in exactly the way I needed to hear it.

And as hard as it was for me, it was harder still for my dad, whose ambitions for me allowed him to overlook the x-rays and the doctors' damning prognoses in the blind hope that there was gridiron glory waiting for me on the other side of all that adversity. I think in some way, he didn't want to give up on a shared dream that at least one "Steve Jones" would fully achieve the athletic success that he'd once tasted briefly but had ultimately been unable to realize for himself as fully as he'd wanted to.

I understand that. And love him for wanting that for me.

But the situation was what it was—and no amount of will power in the world was ever going to change that.

I drove back to Cal Poly knowing that life was about to get much harder.

My parents and I were going to have to face the financial challenges of getting through my last year of college. And, even more than that, I was going to have to give up the one thing that I loved most. My entire life up to that point had centered on nothing but football. It was the only thing that I had ever devoted myself to. It was all I had ever dreamed of doing in my future. It was everything.

And now it was just gone.

I knew then that I was going to have to find a new dream.

Much of what I have to say within these pages is based on the simple premises of finding a dream, stoking the fires of ambition, and then pursuing those goals with absolutely everything that you have—and then finding a little more and trying even harder. And a little harder after that.

I still believe in those simple principles of success and I'm not walking back anything. There is, however, one very important caveat: facts are facts.

Accept them. Do the math. The NFL has thirty-two franchises. There are only fifty-three spots on each team. Some opportunities are finite.

And so, as much as there's a time for pursuing that dream with absolute abandon, there's also a time when you necessarily need to inject a harsh dose of reality into the equation. Sometimes it becomes equally important to reevaluate your dreams.

To regroup. And then press on from there. Maybe in a different direction.

I understand that after everything I put into scholastic athletics, it may appear to some as if I gave up on my dream of playing football in the pros. I assure you all that's not at all what happened.

Sometimes in life you need to change paths. That's not quitting, that's improving your trajectory towards success. I merely reassessed and redirected.

Looking back now I can see everything that I learned from my time playing football. It ingrained in me a certain work ethic and a determination to just keep grinding until I achieved my goals. It also taught me that you can pivot and change directions. That's not failure, that's just adjusting your game plan in order to come out a winner.

And I took that dream of succeeding at the highest levels and elevated it to an even bigger and badder game. The most competitive contest there is: business.

CHAPTER 12
Endure the Hardships

There were a lot of residual complication involved in my walking away from football.

Aside from the game, the sort of lifestyle it had been necessary for me to keep in order to participate at the level I had demanded of myself was the only real framework that I had known throughout my life. While two-a-days and additional hours in the gym had always created significant restrictions in my life, without that ready-made schedule of events, I found some initial difficulty in following a new life pattern that did not revolve around Saturday afternoon game day.

Worst of all, there was some very serious financial fall-out, as well.

Collegiate athletics are by and large a tremendous American enterprise; every year they provide educational opportunities to tens of thousands of student–athletes who otherwise wouldn't be financially able to obtain a Bachelor's degree.

I know this because I was one of those student–athletes.

One of the tragedies built into that system, however, is that when an athlete is injured through no fault of their own and in pursuing the university's competitive interests, the money offered to pursue those educational opportunities is taken away.

"Thanks for playing your heart (and neck) out. Now let's talk about your new financial obligation to the university ..."

The injury to my neck not only took away the football-centered life I'd been living, as well as the NFL dream I had clung to, but it also took away my financial scholarship to Cal Poly. Tuition. Room and board. I had paid for everything with football. Now that account had been closed out.

I suppose it might have been understandable if, at the conclusion of my mad rush for the NFL, I had found some sense of relief and an opportunity for much-needed rest, but my actual experience was the exact opposite of a little well-earned down-time.

Without my scholarship, the dollars and cents of my education became an immediate concern. A seemingly unconquerable obstacle.

My father had worked his ass off every day of his life and there was never a time that he didn't provide for his family. He hadn't, however, planned for the contingency that a day might come in which I wouldn't be able to make my way through college on my own by playing football.

My senior year was a struggle financially. It was also a struggle to find an arena for me to transplant my dream. All of this was so difficult that it took me an additional year to finish the credits I needed to graduate. But I got them.

And while I walked with that degree in political science from Cal Poly (the first one in my family to graduate college), I recognized that the education I'd actually received was far greater than my collegiate coursework. The financial struggles had taught me more about the "real world" workings of this world than anything I'd picked up in my economics classes. The need to forge another workable life plan, to transform what might have been my ultimate defeat into just another rung on the ladder to the success, had schooled me in a difficult life lessons that exposed who I really was.

So, when I collected my diploma, I was understandably proud of the accomplishment of earning that degree. At the same time, however, I was equally aware that I had just completed some (unrecognized) graduate work at the University of Hard Knocks. And they have both proven to be invaluable.

All too often, I hear people complaining about their current situations. What always strikes me at those times is that the individual is simply missing out on the opportunities that are available to them in whatever those supposedly dire circumstances might be.

Sure, hard times often make those opportunities more difficult to see. Trust me, I understand.

Cal Poly is many things, one of them is a destination for many students who find the tuition and related expenses to be no concern at all. And being the odd-guy-out on all of that conspicuous consumption certainly sucked from time to time. (Almost always.) But I never complained. I never let it get me down. I was always looking for the opportunity, for the hole in life's defensive line, the gap that would lead straight to the goal line. And I wasn't shy about taking my hits, dusting myself off, and then hustling back for the next play.

Whatever your circumstances may be—whether you're worried about making it through the day or busy forging an empire (I've been in both spots)—there are opportunities all around you now. Right now.

Hardship is no excuse to give up. Success is no reason to let up. Every day, you have to make the most of what you got and then use that as a foundation to build on.

> **What always strikes me at those times is that the individual is simply missing out on the opportunities that are available to them in whatever those supposedly dire circumstances might be.**

I was lucky enough that after my football prospects were denied, I was able to find something that I loved equally as much. Truth be told, maybe even a little more.

CHAPTER 13
Start Early

When I say that there was something of a socio-economic divide at Cal Poly, I'm not exaggerating. While my buddies spent the time scheduling their trips to Europe or planning their cross-country road trips, I finished up my college days there scrambling to get a job.

And, you know what? I was happy and satisfied for all of us to be doing our own things. I've never understood why some people are filled with bitterness at the success and good fortune of others. To me, that's the sign of a small mind—and an equally small heart.

I was happy for my friends. I wished them all *bon voyage* or whatever was appropriate and waved as they went off. And then I got to work. Literally.

I walked at graduation on a Saturday. I spent Sunday moving my stuff from one apartment to another one. And then on Monday I went to work. (And haven't stopped since.)

At that point, my dad had spent his entire adult life working for Aramark. So had my uncles. An assortment of odd cousins and other more distant relations, too.

> I've never understood why some people are filled with bitterness at the success and good fortune of others. To me, that's the sign of a small mind— and an equally small heart.

In that way, Aramark was very much a "family" business. Not in terms of ownership, obviously, but

69

with regard to what was talked about whenever we got together. On all of those summer camping trips when I was a kid in Livermore, we didn't tell ghost stories or tall tales, we talked about Aramark and the uniform service industry around the campfire. Small talk at kids' birthday parties. The adult table at Thanksgiving. The talk was always about Aramark and the business.

That was just life with the Joneses.

So, after receiving several different job offers during the on-campus interview process at Cal Poly, it seemed like I was destined to follow my family into the industrial laundry and uniform business. It wasn't necessarily what I had wanted, but the pay was good and the training was excellent.

I started in outside sales, working a territory and building it up through cold-calling on potential customers and trying to convince them to switch their providers. Sales. Nothing fancy. But I went to work with all the intensity that I had displayed during my football career. In fact, I viewed each potential sale like a football game; someone was going to win and someone was going to lose. I was determined to be the one that came out on top. Every time. I knew no one was ever going to outwork or out-grind me.

But this time, I had something more than my sheer will. I had all of the knowledge that I needed to be successful. I had been trained in the business since I was a kid. I had worked at Aramark every summer since I was a freshman in high school, washing trucks, counting shop towels, rolling mats, sorting through dirty laundry, going on deliveries and sales calls. I knew the industrial uniform and laundry business through my own hard work and through a lifetime of family discussions. I knew the Aramark playbook like the back of my hand.

While others struggled to gain traction and new sales, I outworked everyone and was selling new accounts at a record pace.

When receptionists walled off their bosses from me or kept me hanging on the phone all day or met me with a curt, "He can't be disturbed right now!" I learned to be at the shop at five or six in the morning when that old-school boss was showing up to work and there was plenty of time to talk about "the good ol' days," his business—and his order.

I quickly found in sales a similar sort of excitement like that I had found out on the football field. Every sale was cause for a moment's celebration, but then a burning desire (need?) to get right back at it and make another sale. A bigger sale.

And another.

Day in and day out, that level of commitment—and the sales it generated—got noticed by the company. I was promoted in a year and a half to run sales all the way out in San Bernardino.

Within a year after that promotion, I was called up to run all of the sales teams throughout all of Southern California. I had responsibility for growing three major areas: Los Angeles, San Diego, and San Bernardino. During my first year in this capacity of running all of the sales for the region, I took the region from the worst in the country to third best in the US.

My career was really taking off. I was receiving huge recognition within the company and being actively recruited by everyone inside and outside the industry.

Despite all the success, however, I couldn't hide from myself that I was searching for something more.

CHAPTER 14
Do What You Love

I still had a dream, but I confess that at the time I was maybe a little less certain about the specifics of my goal.

Finding another dream was something I was confident I would do, but there were some moments when not having a set plan for the future locked down and in place caused me a moment or two of personal doubt. It was during those moments that I began to think about the plans and ambitions of others. (Always a mistake.)

For my fellow Political Science majors at Cal Poly, the most popular after-school plan was to head to law school, spend three more years there, and then cash in on the non-stop gravy train of a big firm in LA or Orange County. I have to admit that this sounded like a perfectly fine plan and—not having a personal goal of my own at the time—I was willing to pick it up and see just how far I could run with it.

At the time, I was dating a young woman whose father owned all of the Del Tacos. While that might not necessarily translate across much of the country today, in Southern California and throughout the Southwest in the 1990s, Del Taco was *huge*!

One weekend she took me back to her home, an incredible mansion in Newport Beach, to meet him. Mr. Baker was smart and polished and he carried himself with the same sort of refined confidence that my mentor, Mr. Roberson, did. He was exactly the sort of man that I wanted to emulate.

He shook my hand and we got to talking. Understandably, as I was dating his daughter at the time, the subject of my future plans happened to come up. I breathed a sigh of relief, knowing I had this one covered and said confidently, "I'm planning on going to law school, sir."

The smile dropped from his face. "Why?"

I'd thought "law school" was the answer to the question every girl's father had on his mind and so this follow-up caught me a little off guard.

Without thinking too much about it, I offered what I thought was the most obvious response. "Because lawyers are rich."

His face fell further. "Some people do make money at the law," he said. "But for every rich lawyer out there, I'll show you two that are busting a gut just to cover the bills this month—and I'll throw in another that's not going to cover those expenses at all. No, if you want to go to law school, I think that's a fine thing. But go because you love the law and you think you can make a difference in the world, not just because you think you'll make money. That's not the way to do anything." I nodded like I understood. "And it's no sin not to know what you want to do with your life at your age." He laughed to himself. "Hell, at my age either. You've already got a fine job, work for a while. Go get another if you want. Go back to school and pick up an MBA. But make sure that whatever you end up doing is something that you really love or you'll never realize real success. You might make money, but trust me, it won't feel like real success unless you love it."

"Yes, sir."

He redirected his question. "Now what do you love?"

Besides football, there was something else that had managed to earn a place in my heart over the years. "I think what I'd like to do is own an In-N-Out Burger. Maybe a couple of stores."

He didn't dismiss my idea as immature, as I might have expected. Instead, he nodded as he considered the proposition. "Well, I tell you what. In-N-Out is family-owned right now, no franchises available. But I tell you what. You go out and get yourself a job at an In-N-Out, you learn that business from the grease traps on up to the manager's office, you put in your time and show me that you have the dedication and determination—and the *love*—to make that dream come true and I will back you all the way. You come back to me after you've accomplished that and we'll start up Steve's Burgers and we'll go start our own franchise."

I never did take him up on that kind offer, but I didn't forget it either.

Beyond being unbelievably generous, every word he spoke was the truth. I never went to law school. And there is no Steve's Burgers along the strip of fast food franchises in your town, for a very good reason.

It wasn't that I lacked the dedication or commitment or that I was short on ideas or backing. The simple fact of it is that I didn't have the love in my heart. What I had done throughout my football career, I was able to do only because I truly loved the game.

The key to success in any endeavor is to find something that you love, something that you can totally devote yourself to. If it's not an act of love, a passionate commitment of everything that you are, then it just won't work the way you want it to.

If I was ever judgmental in my youth about teammates who didn't give their all or wound up walking away from the game, I regret those opinions now because I understand that they simply didn't have the love that's necessary for any of us to do the extraordinary things that are required to achieve true success in a life that is quick to offer participation trophies of mediocrity to all of those who are willing to settle.

Whatever course you take in this world, it cannot be the one that only leads to money. And neither can it be the path that you think others want you to take or that you feel some obligation to trudge down. None of those will ever lead you where you really want to go. Not really.

The key to success in any endeavor is to find something that you love, something that you can totally devote yourself to. If it's not an act of love, a passionate commitment of everything that you are, then it just won't work the way you want it to.

CHAPTER 15
Find Your Reason

While I was busy working my way up the ladder in corporate America, I got a phone call one day.

That's not quite accurate. It wasn't just *any* phone call. It was *the* phone call. The phone call that I'd given up on ever receiving.

One afternoon, my phone rang and instead of the customer or sales lead whom I might have expected, it was my former coach from Saddleback Junior College. He remembered me—not just as the guy who had thrown up on his shoes, but as the gridiron madman who had played offense and defense and special teams. Every snap of every game.

Coach had just taken a coaching position in the NFL's newest scouting program, the World Football League in Europe. He wanted me to come try out for the team.

And there it was. An offer to play professional football. In Europe. As part of a developmental program that was specifically designed to channel players into the NFL.

It was everything I could have dreamed of. And more. But now that I'd received it, I wasn't quite sure.

Letting go of my dream to play in the pros hadn't been easy. And so, the possibility—the temptation—was painfully strong at a time when I had just started to make some headway in redesigning my life without football.

I called my dad. He wasn't nearly as happy as I thought he'd be. (Looking back at it now, I think it must have been painful for him, too.)

"What are you going to do?" he asked.

"I gotta try, don't I?"

My father was a poker-faced guy, but I could tell that wasn't the answer he'd hoped for. "You don't have to do anything you don't want to do. You've worked too damn hard to make sure of that."

"But, Dad, I—we—worked so hard to—"

"You have worked hard. And just look what you've achieved already. You got your degree. You got a great job. You're doing so well that soon you're going to have an even better job. You've got so much right now, I think you ought to think hard before you throw that all away just to chase—"

"It was my dream. Our dream."

"You're in your twenties and you walk like an eighty-year-old man." We both laughed, because it was true. "When I signed with the Pirates," he continued, " in 1962, I was twenty-two years old. I signed a contract for $58,000—I don't have the faintest idea what that's worth today—but it's a helluva lot money now and it was a whole helluva lot more back then. I thought I had everything, you know?"

I smiled at the story that I'd heard ten thousand times, the one that had been the hot ember which had ignited my own dream. But I'd never heard the next part before.

"Hearing my name getting called over the loudspeaker as I came up to bat. Kids wanting my autograph. Rubbing shoulders with Clemente and Stargell and Mazeroski. It was all great. But, in my whole life, do you know when I was the proudest?" I didn't. "Every goddamn time you took the field."

I didn't know what to say.

"There's a time for young men to pursue their dreams of glory, but that's all they are. And there's a greater reward in this life than something as fleeting as glory. Trust me. You got your degree. You got a great job that you're excelling at. You're on the track for something bigger than the NFL. And when a boy of your own suits up and steps out onto the field, you'll know exactly what I mean. And you'll see that I was right about this. It's time to be a man."

You need to do something that you love. That sort of passion is absolutely indispensable. But it's not enough. You need something more. A reason.

I called my coach up and thanked him for the amazing opportunity, but I never tried out for the team. I listened to my dad. I'm damn glad that I did.

You need to do something that you love. That sort of passion is absolutely indispensable. But it's not enough. You need something more. A reason. No matter how much you love something, you need a reason to keep doing it.

I loved football, but I understood in that moment that it was my love for my father, for my entire family, that kept me at it. It was never just about me. It was always something bigger than that.

When I hung up the phone with my former coach, I went back to work. Not just because I loved it, but because I understood for the first time that I was building something meant for more than just me, something bigger than me.

And that was when I *really* got busy.

CHAPTER 16
Get an Ownership Interest

I had achieved so much in the industrial uniform industry in my first three years and I had myriad opportunities being presented to me: go on a path to be a general manager, go on a path to training, or work my way up into the corporate structure.

At the same time, following my family into the uniform industry wasn't what I wanted to be doing.

For starters, everyone within the company knew who my father was. I was always introduced as Little Steve (at 6'2") because my father was already known as Big Steve.

Despite the fact that I had made my own career through my own hard work, I knew there were those within the company and throughout the industry who thought it was because of who my family was.

My career was going great and I easily could have chosen a path that would have led to its own success, but I wanted to do something different. I wanted to make a name for myself, go to a company in an industry where no one knew my name, or more importantly who my family was. I decided it was time to leave the "family" business.

I had several companies reaching out to me, multiple competitors in the industrial uniform industry. There were also offers to sell communication equipment for AT&T, selling commercial aircraft for Boeing, and lots of industrial companies that depended on business-to-business sales and relationships to drive their growth.

The most interesting offer, however, came from Browning Ferris Industries or BFI Waste Services, the second-largest trash company in the world, behind only Waste Management.

I was intrigued that such a blue-collar industry could be so big and professional.

BFI and Waste Management were changing the industry and rolling up all of the mom-and-pop trash companies and combining them all into a serious multi-billion-dollar business.

BFI, particularly, was growing and the opportunities they offered were huge. I decided that this was where I wanted to challenge myself next and where I could compete in a major corporate environment and make a name for myself completely on my own terms.

I took the position with BFI as a district sales and marketing manager. Again, I was put in charge of marketing and sales for Southern California. I also had responsibility over client retention. I was the head of a large sales department as well as service and retention managers. It was all fairly familiar ground and as a result, the transition came very naturally to me.

It was just like any other service industry and I found that much of what I had learned in perfecting my sales game in the industrial uniform industry was freely transferable to my new position. Sales in the service industry is all about relationships. People want to do business with people that they like. It's just that simple.

If I hadn't already learned that lesson (and I *had*) I would have learned it from the "old-school crew" that hung around the BFI offices.

BFI was a huge corporation with annual revenues somewhere north of $7 billion, but they had built themselves up to that size in no small part by acquiring any number of smaller waste companies.

These weren't the posh corporations that BFI had morphed into. No, these were junkyards and landfills, scrapyards and trash heaps.

The old guys who had started these gold mines of garbage, who had begun their careers running crappy, old trucks all around Southern California and then made a fortune selling out to BFI, they all hung out at the parent company regional headquarters. They spent their days swapping stories and I loved to listen in whenever I had the time and opportunity. They were a treasure trove of information and entertaining stories.

None of the other young bucks recognized the value to be gained from tapping the collective experience and knowledge of this group of old-school guys, but I saw it all right away.

Every one of them was a character in the very best way possible. Their payout had made them all millionaires, but they were still the rough-around-the edges guys they'd been when they started out in those crappy trucks all those years ago.

No matter how complicated you want to make business, the realities are very simple: you're either an owner or an employee. Those are the only two options.

And that was the most important lesson that I learned from them. If you want to take the fullest advantage of the opportunities available to you in the business world, you have to have an ownership interest.

No matter how complicated you want to make business, the realities are very simple: you're either an owner or an employee. Those are the only two options.

It doesn't matter how great your package is, if you're an employee, your rewards are limited. By your contract. By the available hours you can work. Whatever it is, there are limitations on your situation.

If you want to maximize your returns, then you have to have an ownership interest.

And that lesson sent me off on a new course altogether.

CHAPTER 17
Check the Boxes

I was BFI's district sales manager for all of Southern California. I was just in my mid-twenties. Yet, I still wasn't satisfied. I wanted something more.

And because I wasn't sure just exactly what that was, I settled on graduate school.

I know that maybe doesn't make a whole lot of sense, but I knew that I wanted to get a MBA at some point in time. Or, at least, I knew I wanted to *have* one. Whatever I did or didn't do with it, getting an MBA was just one of those boxes that I wanted to check. What better time was there for me to go back to school than when I was already working sixty-plus hours a week and had just taken over one of the largest territories that BFI, this seven-billion-dollar company, had on their books.

There was, of course, no chance for me to go back to school full-time, so I had looked at the night school programs in area universities. USC and Pepperdine had two of the best. Excellent programs, both of them. I applied and got into them both.

The problem was that the tuition for each school was around thirty grand a year and my boss wouldn't approve the tuition reimbursement for either program at that price point.

I asked him what he would approve and he replied with a curt, "Half that."

That was what I had: an interest in getting an MBA and about half of the financial backing I needed to get one.

Eventually, I found a program at the University of Redlands that was as highly regarded, but wasn't nearly as expensive as the other programs I had looked at. Still, the school was a small private university with a good reputation and would provide me with the chance to achieve another dream: getting a Master's degree; something no one in my family had ever accomplished.

The next thing I knew I was a graduate student at Redlands.

It's one thing to be a college student when your day-to-day focus is on academics. It's another thing altogether to be a graduate student when your day-to-day is ... well, your day-to-day and everything else, including the academics, have to be shoehorned into the spare time you just don't have.

My days still started at 6:00 or 7:00 a.m. And they still ran twelve to fourteen hours a piece. But now I was running out to Redlands and working on class projects at night and on the weekends.

The thing about getting an MBA is that the great majority of the coursework is participating in group projects. And so much of my time was spent coordinating my efforts with others in my class. It wasn't all that much different from running a defense.

I spent three years like that. Working sixty hours plus at BFI. Tuesday and Thursday nights in class. Weekends trying to herd my classmates into an endless series of oral presentations and partnered papers.

Three years later I had an MBA—but no exact reason as to *why*.

In the end, I knew that what I really wanted to be was a CEO. I wanted to be like Mr. Roberson. And Mr. Baker. I wanted to be the quarterback of a new kind of team.

I knew that whatever I eventually used my MBA for, there was a distinct possibility that *not* having the degree might be a significant-enough obstacle in reaching the places I wanted to go and achieving the sort of ends I had roughly in mind.

I wanted people to be able to look at my resume and see that, if nothing else, I had checked that box. So, in the end, all of the sacrifice and hard work was well worth it. Not because I had a specific idea of what I was going to use it for, but because it prepared me for whatever I wanted to do.

Preparing yourself for your future should be a constant consideration in your present state. Whether or not you've arrived at a specific goal, you should always be working to better yourself.

Read. Make new connections and tend to the ones that you've already established. Get the degree. Do whatever you think might advance you. Be willing to pay the price for success, be willing to go through the grind.

Then, when you find that goal, and feel that purpose, you'll be prepared.

> **Preparing yourself for your future should be a constant consideration in your present state. Whether or not you've arrived at a specific goal, you should always be working to better yourself.**

CHAPTER 18
Follow That Dream

The irony of my graduate school experience was that by the time I was through with my MBA, I was also through with BFI. It wasn't that it wasn't a great position. It was. I was the sales leader running the sales and customer service teams in a billion-dollar region. And it wasn't that I wasn't meeting the hefty expectations that corporate had placed on my shoulders. I was exceeding them.

My decision was based simply on the fact that I knew I could never find at BFI what I really wanted most: ownership.

That situation simply wasn't going to happen for me at BFI. Or, at least, not at the level that I wanted for my future. BFI was already a multi-billion-dollar enterprise, there was no room for Steve Jones to come in and reorganize it the way he wanted and build it up.

And building my own company from the bottom up was my new—highly-defined—dream.

When I turned in my notice at BFI, the news of my imminent departure created some very deep ripples in the corporate pond. Before I knew it, I was booked on a flight to Houston to meet with Bruce Ranck, BFI's CEO. BFI had an entire corporate tower in downtown Houston. I was scheduled for a breakfast meeting with Mr. Ranck, so I was escorted up to the very top of the building, where there was an executive dining room.

It was early in the morning and I was waiting for Mr. Ranck, just looking out over the Houston skyline as the sun was coming up. Breathtaking.

All of a sudden, I heard Mr. Ranck behind me. "Someday all of this could be yours."

In that moment everything became crystal clear.

Most people would have heard those encouraging words and immediately rethought their plans to leave the company. A comment like that from the big boss is what almost every corporate player dreams of throughout their career. But not me.

It wasn't that I was ungrateful or unappreciative of all the opportunities that BFI had offered me. And I certainly understood the unspoken promise that our meeting was meant to convey. I was aware of it all. But what resonated with me most at that moment was that I didn't want a promise that at some day in a future beyond my control someone else would "give" me anything.

I wanted all of that, but I wanted it on my terms, including my timeline. I didn't want my future to be some arbitrary consideration—my football career had already taught me the painful lesson about waiting for "someday."

I wanted to start working for that future right away, grinding like I always had for everything else. I wanted my future on my terms and I wanted it always to be a part of my present state. I wanted every early morning and each late night to be a part of my future.

And so, the great irony was that Mr. Ranck's kind words, which were meant to address my unrest and draw me back into the corporate fold at BFI, were exactly the words I needed to convince myself that I was absolutely doing the right thing by leaving.

It was time. Time to get grinding on my future.

CHAPTER 19
Don't Look Back

I left BFI and the matching 401(k), the supplemental retirement plan, and all of the other corporate goodies that I had become accustomed to while working for them. I took all of that and traded it in for a position at a small, family-run company called Universal Protection Service.

When I joined the company, their annual revenues were maybe $12 million. Not any more than that. They didn't offer even the most basic 401(k), not even a fundamental pension.

For any outside observer, I understood that this seemed like a losing proposition. There was almost nothing about the company that anyone would have seen as attractive. In fact, there wasn't much more to Universal than the bare bones of a company, so I understood people's skepticism.

I, however, saw something different, something more. I saw: potential. More than anyone else, I was painfully well aware of everything that Universal was not, but I was absolutely certain I could build it into something far, far more.

That was exactly what I was looking for; not a move-in-ready position, but a fix-it-upper that I could remodel according to my vision to create something all my own.

I was always aware, however, that achieving that goal was going to be a hell of a lot of hard work. Still, as I've said, most everyone I shared my future plans with could not see the vision I saw for Universal. And it wasn't simply the company that people saw as a mistake. Once I'd announced my intentions to enter the security industry, I was surprised to discover that there were some individuals outside of that field who held a certain disdain for the entire industry. (Keep in mind that this was with me coming from the waste management industry.)

I remember a conversation with one gentleman who couldn't believe my decision to leave BFI for Universal. He asked me point-blank, "You're leaving your position to go manage monkeys?"

I had no idea what he was talking about. "Excuse me?"

"You're going to be managing knuckleheads. That ragtag security company, those five-dollars-an-hour security guards; it's going to be like managing knuckleheads."

I shrugged off his comments, not to agree with him, but to dismiss him entirely. "No," I said. "I'm leaving this job to start a career. Mark my words, just like BFI is a billion-dollar enterprise, I'll turn that 'ragtag security company' into a billion-dollar enterprise too."

He smirked. "You can't possibly believe that."

"I can. And I do. Just watch me."

I'm still waiting for him to reach out and tell me that I was right and he was wrong.

People will always have opinions. Weigh their words and consider their counsel.

I've learned plenty in schools and from reading, but the bulk of my real education has come from listening to others. The advice that mentors have imparted to me along the way has been invaluable. And I have always found gold in the stories that people like to tell, whether it was my father and his family sharing Aramark stories around a campfire or the crew of old-school guys swapping tales at BFI.

At the same time, I have always been aware that among those who will offer you valuable insight, there are others whose only intention is to try to inject your dreams with their own doubt and fear and negativity. I never listened to a word that guy—or anyone like him—had to say.

I knew what I was getting into with Universal. I had done my homework and I wasn't concerned with those who couldn't see all of the opportunities that I could.

Consider what people have to tell you, but never let them make the decision for you. Getting as many opinions as you can is often helpful, but do your own due diligence so that you know the answer for yourself.

Getting as many opinions as you can is often helpful, but do your own due diligence so that you know the answer for yourself.

I was aware of everything I was leaving behind at BFI. More to the point, I knew that BFI had a strict no-re-hire policy in place. There was no swinging door. Once I was out, I was out to stay. I knew that and I went anyway. I knew what I was going to do and I never looked back.

Never look back.

CHAPTER 20
Take the Risk, But Don't Gamble

Let me step away from the narrative for a moment to directly address something of considerable importance. I've talked in these pages a lot about risk and, believe me, I have a whole lot more to say on the subject as it had factored into my career.

Let's stop for a moment to consider the very nature of risk—a crucial meditation that I think a lot of people overlook and fail to complete before assessing whatever situation may confront them and then taking the appropriate action.

Risk is an inherent component of every endeavor, both in our personal lives and our professional careers. It simply can't be avoided. Because the yin-yang nature of the universe almost demands that every benefit be accompanied by the possibility of some loss or setback, every action carries with it some relative risk. Even "playing it safe" and taking no action at all, goes hand in hand with the (often sizable) risk of missed opportunities.

No matter what any of us do, our lives are almost necessarily just a series of interconnected risks.

I think that's a good thing. A great thing.

In my life, I have always gone out of my way to embrace the risks that I have encountered, not because I am in any way foolhardy or reckless; just the opposite. I have always been comfortable with—maybe even sought out—situations rife with risk, because I know that they alone offer incredible moments of advancement, the opportunity to take significant steps toward the future, and to reap rewards

I have always been comfortable with— maybe even sought out—situations rife with risk, because I know that they alone offer incredible moments of advancement, the opportunity to take significant steps toward the future, and to reap rewards that make the struggle involved in your endeavors all worthwhile.

that make the struggle involved in your endeavors all worthwhile.

Stepping out on the field to play football was a risk, particularly after my string of injuries. Going to Cal Poly and putting myself in a position where I had to rise above the sort of academic standards that I hadn't even considered before was a risk. And, certainly, leaving the corporate comforts of BFI to take a position with a family-run security business—when I was very definitely *not* family—was an enormous risk.

At the same time, consider the above in light of the fact that I had been playing football since I could walk, I'd worked my butt off in every practice I'd ever attended, and I knew my teams' playbooks like they were the Bible and I was a Gospel-quoting preacher. Most important of all, I knew I had the talent and drive to succeed out on the field.

I walked into Cal Poly aware (and remorseful) that I had never dedicated myself to academics the way I had to athletics, but I knew I was in the hands of some of the greatest educators in the country. And I knew that I had the intelligence and dedication to succeed in my coursework if only I approached it like I had gone after my dream to play football.

The same was true with my decision to take the position with Universal Protection Service. I was young and single and aware of the fact that if there were any negative results in the road ahead of me, I could bounce back from them very quickly and without anyone besides myself being affected by them. I had a solid academic background. I had a certain corporate pedigree behind me. And I had skills that I knew that I could take to any other industry in any other region of the country and not only go to work but continue to succeed like I had with my previous positions.

My point is that going to work at Universal Protection Service might have been a risk, but it was not a gamble. There's an all-important distinction to be made there.

A risk is a calculated move that is balanced against your own assessment of the situation and your reasonable expectation that your capabilities (i.e., intelligence, special skills, connections, whatever) will enable you to reap the benefits to be gained and that whatever adverse results might be experienced will not negatively impact you to a point of severity that would cripple your overall life quest. Risk is something that you can assess, calculate a plan to handle, and then execute on that.

A gamble is something very different. A gamble is walking into a casino and putting money down on an event that you can't assess or control. The roll of the dice. The turn of the card. Whatever. A gamble is doing something or facing some consequence … well, just because.

I suppose there's some psychological or biological explanation behind that sort of behavior. Endorphins. Or Jungian struggles. Or something. I don't pretend to fully understand. My point is that I take risks all damn day, but I very rarely gamble. And I absolutely never gamble in my business affairs.

When I sat down to write this book, one of the driving motivations I held was that my words—and the life experiences that I captured with them—might find their way to some young woman or man who was looking for some guidance and mentoring, like I once was. Maybe someone who felt trapped and confined in a job that hadn't evolved into a career would find in these pages the necessary spark to reignite their passions and double down on their efforts to make their dreams the core realities of their lives.

I wanted to provide the sort of positive influence that has always been a strong motivator for me. For that reason, I would deeply regret if a reader were to misinterpret these same words as an invitation to take something as precious as one's future and leave it all up to the whims of fate to decide the outcome.

If someone wants to go out and start a business, I think that's great … if they know the industry inside-out, they completely understand all of the moving parts of that business, and they are certain that they have all of the resources (including their own dedication) to get that enterprise off of the ground and make it a real and thriving concern. Otherwise, it's a gamble; one that could wipe out and obliterate any and all future opportunities.

If someone has a job that doesn't satisfy them and they want to start over in another position or entirely new career, I think that's great … if they've done the calculations to determine that the planned move will produce the desired results, all of the other expected change impacts won't adversely affect their personal responsibilities, and they're absolutely committed to whatever hard work and sacrifice will be necessary to make the situation work. Otherwise, jumping ship midstream is a gamble that could result in a long swim to the other side. Or, even worse, sinking like a stone.

My point and the long and short of it is that there are no shortcuts to success. None. Certainly, gambling is not a viable option.

There's a reason that "The House" always wins.

This book of mine should absolutely be read as an open invitation to realizing success and as an accompanying how-to manual for calculated action and determined actions necessary to make that happen. It should not, however, be seen as an excuse for recklessness.

My decision to leave BFI for a position with Universal Protection Service was absolutely a risk. But it was never a gamble.

And the story that follows, the chronicles of how that company evolved over the years, is certainly filled with accounts of the significant risks that I (and my partner) took in order to make the transition of that business a reality.

None of that success, however, would have been possible if I hadn't first done the homework necessary to fully assess all of the situational possibilities and implications and then worked to meet them head-on with the day-after-day grind required to make certain that the eventual results were in line with our reasonable expectations.

There was never any real question, the results were always guaranteed.

That's the lesson to take away from the tale. Take the risk, but never gamble.

CHAPTER 21
Get Ready to Run

So, even though moving from BFI to Universal Protection Service was admittedly a risk, it was a calculated one and I was certain that I could make it all work out—not just for myself, but for everyone involved, including the folks hiring me.

The Universal headquarters were located in an unassuming building in an industrial section of Orange, California. The interior of the building was nice enough, but it was a far cry from the corporate luxury of BFI's penthouse executive dining room that I still remembered from my last trip to Houston. In fact, Universal offered none of what I'd come to regard as the standard executive accommodations inside their utilitarian headquarters, including the sort of technology that I'd gotten used to as a tool of the trade at BFI.

My simple request for a laptop—something I'd been using since my undergraduate days at Cal Poly and that was fairly commonplace by this time—was regarded as some sort of futuristic request in an organization in which only the accountants and the receptionists had even desktop computers in their offices. When I joined the team at Universal, everything from employee scheduling to incident reports was still done the exact same way it had been when the company was first founded thirty-four years earlier: on paper and by hand. So, even before I began to roll up my sleeves and get down to work on my very first day, I knew that I was going to have my hands full in just bringing the business into the modern age.

As it happened, that very first day on the job started for me with a meeting with the company's president, Brian Cescolini. Great guy. Brian had come into the business as a security guard and over the course of his twenty-four years with Universal, he'd been able to work his way up to the very top of the corporate ladder through his hard work, dedication, and ambition.

Under Brian's guidance, Universal Protection had grown slowly to become a company with annual revenues in the range of $10 to $12 million. It was an admirable job and showed the potential for future growth, but the company had hit an earnings plateau at that point and, despite all of their best interests and efforts, they really couldn't find a way to accelerate beyond that.

That was where I came in. I was brought in to make the changes necessary to get the company up and over that particular obstacle.

My initial meeting with Brian went just fine. I think that almost instantly there was a certain personal chemistry between us and, even more important, a definite business synergy that we were both aware had the potential to produce some real results for us personally and for the company as a whole. That very first day, Brian had scheduled a lunch meeting with some representatives from the Irvine Company, which at the time was our very biggest client.

Brian is ... an excitable guy from time to time ... and just the ride to the restaurant through Orange County traffic was an adventure in itself. We arrived at the restaurant (no small miracle there) and met the rest of our party, folks from the Irvine Company, who at the time were Universal's biggest and most important client. Brian introduced me to everyone, including the property manager.

Then he turned and gestured to me like I was the showcase grand prize on a gameshow. "This is Steve. We just brought him on board. He's a bright young man and he's going to help us bring the company into the future. Everything we've done for you to-date, we're soon going to be able to do for you so much better."

The property manager smiled like it pained her and then said to me. "I'm sorry to do this to you on your very first day, but we've been with Universal for some time now and we thought it was important to meet with you in person to let you know that we've decided to cancel our contract with you."

Her announcement seemed to stop time and suck all of the sound out of the room. Everything stopped. Not even half way through my very first day and my company's very biggest client had decided to give us our walking papers. No one knew what to do, including Brian.

The silence and the awkwardness were excruciating. In the midst of it all, I realized that if someone was going to do something to fix things, it was going to fall on me. Even at that point, I had been in business long enough to realize that there were a number of ways that people in my position might react to such a situation. The first would be just a passive acceptance of their decision. "We're sorry to hear this, but we respect your decision." Another—and one that I've found is far too common with many people in business, even among executives at the highest level—would have been to play the (passive-aggressive) victim game. "Really? After everything we've done for you over the years, this is how you end things?" The third, I suppose, would have been just plain aggressive. "This is b.s.!"

I didn't make any of those plays.

I certainly wasn't going to simply accept the fact that the most important client to the company I had just joined (and what I intended to one day have an ownership interest in) was going to walk out on our lunch and take their business with them. But I wasn't going to plead either. Pleading never works, not really. I certainly wasn't going to get angry. Anger never works either. Absolutely never.

What I did do was to take a breath and think. Then I made a statement that I knew would be persuasive because it was absolutely, 100 percent true. My words weren't terribly impassioned, just direct and to the point. "This is my first day. I don't know you and you don't know me. But I will tell you that I'm smart and an extremely hard worker and I need you to give me thirty days to fix this. If you'll tell me why you've reached this decision, what exactly you're dissatisfied with, and I don't fix it for you within thirty days, you can always terminate us then. In the long run, thirty days won't matter to you one way or another. But if you just walk away right now without giving me this opportunity to repair our relationship, then you're going to be walking away from the company that is going to set the standard in the security industry—a security company that is going to be completely devoted to exceeding all of your expectations from here on in."

That was everything I had to say on the subject. Everything that had to be said.

The property manager was so impressed by my direct, no-nonsense handling of a situation that might have triggered some other young executive into a panic that she gave me those thirty days I'd asked for.

I took full advantage of the opportunity. The first thing I did was to sit down to a conference with their representatives and ask them to let me know everything that had left them dissatisfied with our company and the services we provided to them. It was a very long conversation. Long, but absolutely necessary. And incredibly beneficial to me.

Even today I am amazed by people in business who hide away from the problems in their own organizations, who cover their ears to the complaints so they won't hear the bad news. Sure, everyone likes to hear compliments and receive praise, but there's little value in those kind words. The information that every business really needs lies within the complaints.

The information that every business really needs lies within the complaints.

I sat down with the people from the Irvine Company and they told me everything that I needed to fix at Universal.

All in all, the fixes were easy enough. They had concerns about our lack of modern technology, but that was an issue I'd already had my eye on since the first moment I walked into my computer-less office and realized that simply having a company cell phone was regarded by the owners as a modern indulgence. Their other main complaint centered on a lack of customer service. I understood that one too. Many of the managerial positions at Universal had come to be filled by former security guards who, like Brian, had worked their way up and out of the overnight patrol and earned a seat behind a desk.

Unlike Brian, however, far too many of these guys had made that advancement without ever tailoring their behavior and attitudes to meet their new positions. They were a little rough around the edges and not necessarily trained in providing the sort of customer service interface that I knew was necessary to keep and build a customer base.

I might have been new to the security industry, but I was already enough of a veteran of the service sector that I knew that everything was based on the relationships forged with clients. It amazed me then and still astounds me how many players in the game fail to recognize that so much of success in business is based on the level of customer service that you can offer. It seems so simple to me, given that it's right there in the name.

Take it from me, the key to success in the service industry—and I think any industry, and life itself—is building real relationships. That's everything.

I sat down with the property manager from the Irvine Company and listened to what she had to say, the good and the bad—but especially the bad. And then I took active steps to address every complaint she had, to make sure the Universal Protection met every reasonable expectation she could hold for us. Just like I'd promised.

And at the end of thirty days, I'd not only changed her mind about terminating our contract, but I'd managed to establish a relationship between us that secured that contract into the future. More than that, I'd developed a relationship with someone who turned out to be a strong advocate for me and my company and whom I consider to be a personal friend to this day.

But that wasn't the end of it. Not at all.

If the Irvine Company, our largest and most important client, had issues with our service that were serious enough to drive them to the brink of cancelling our contract permanently, then I was relatively certain that all of our clients had problems with us.

Day after day, I reached out to every one of our customers and set up meeting after meeting, talking to every client until I was certain that I knew what problems existed with each and every contract and within our organization, in general. And then I took all of the comments I had acquired and set out a plan of action to address them all. I went through the list methodically and I didn't stop until I had taken all of the steps necessary to correct each and every one of them.

Of course, making all of these reformations in our operations wasn't necessarily an easy thing to do. That wasn't necessarily because the steps themselves were difficult, but because the owners of the company were often reluctant to follow my recommendations about what was necessary to cure these areas of concern.

Universal Protection was, as I've said before, very much a family-owned enterprise and that whole nepotistic mind-set permeated every aspect of the company. When I offered my suggestions that some of the old-school guys they'd started out with had been put into positions that were really beyond their capabilities, the owners were often more than a little resistant to make the suggested replacements that were necessary to provide for the more professional and polished customer–client interface that I knew the company needed. Often, the owner's resistance turned to outright refusal when the employees I identified for replacement were actually family members by blood or marriage.

While I appreciated their loyalty, maybe even shared a bit of it in my heart, the business reality of the situation was that we needed to build a team, a cohesive unit that could not only understand the increasingly sophisticated aspects of what had once been a rather simple, "old school" business, but was also capable of taking care of all of our customers—and, more importantly, attracting new ones.

The debate went back and forth for a while, but eventually I was finally able to convey to the owners the soundness (and necessity) of my restructuring goals.

For my first hire, I brought aboard a guy I had previously worked with at BFI. Like me, he had never worked in the security industry before, but he was a quality guy and I knew that he not only understood what I wanted to accomplish but was also more than capable of doing his share to make sure that it got done. And with that one addition, we went on a tear. In my first year there, we took the company from the $12 million plateau that Universal had been stuck at for a number of years and grew the business to $16 million. That growth—more than 30 percent—was the largest the company had seen in its existence.

That substantial increase in annual revenues amounted to a return that was far more significant than either of the owners had expected when they first brought me into the company. But it was more than just those revenue numbers that my team was posting. We were also building real relationships throughout our territory that were already beginning to generate real leads.

Real relationships. Real leads.

We were defining the new standard in security guard services, but I knew that in order to maximize the opportunities that were presenting themselves and continue our exceptional growth, I needed to create a real sales force to facilitate Universal branching out into territories that we'd never even contemplated expanding into before this.

The owners, however, were not fans of what they considered to be just another of my revolutionary ideas. "Sales people don't tend to work in this industry," they told me.

I didn't know what to say. "Hmmm, that's interesting, because they work in absolutely every other industry. They work in the industrial uniform industry. They work in the waste management industry. Our competitors in this industry seem to have sales people working for them and that seems to be working just fine for them."

They were not persuaded. "We've got people here in the office that handle any calls coming in from would-be customers."

"But people don't want to just call in and talk to a stranger," I assured them. "People want to do business with a company they have confidence in, a company they trust—especially in an industry that provides security. I think if you hired a competent sales force and dedicated professionals, you'd see that they could develop important relationships and be very successful for us, as well."

They shook their heads. "We've already tried sales people and they just didn't work out for us."

I knew that what they really meant was that they'd tried to plug one relative or another into the position, without the particular talent, training, or support necessary to be successful. "I think we need to try again," I said. "I think the company is at a position where we need to put together a real sales force. Professionals who can build relationships, not just take orders."

Neither owner was personally persuaded by the argument I'd offered in support of my position, but the success I'd already demonstrated the previous year finally earned me this one concession.

But just one concession. I was authorized to hire a single salesman.

It wasn't what I wanted, but I considered the addition a major victory on my part. And, as it happened, I knew exactly who I wanted to fill out that slot.

I had met the guy back in my industrial uniform days and—with the single exception of myself—he was the best salesman I had ever come across in my time there. I called him up and convinced him that if he came over to Universal, the opportunities and potential were absolutely limitless. (I told you I was the best salesman.)

The first year with Universal, our new salesman exceeded any reasonable expectations and chalked up sales in excess of $6 million.

That was an enormous contribution to our efforts to grow the business.

In just over two years with the company, my customer service-based approach to the business, the introduction of technology, some internal restructuring, and the creation of an actual functioning sales force (even if that was only one guy) had driven the company's revenues from that $12 million plateau to well over $20 million.

At the end of my third year, we were approaching $25 million in revenue.

The company was really rolling. It was spreading into new markets that we'd never thought of venturing into before. And all of this growth was attracting attention within the industry. People were talking about Universal Protection.

All in all, I would've thought that these results were a positive indicator of the type of potential we had in the company. But for the two guys who had started the company and had never shown any real interest in seeing it as anything more than a small, family-owned company, more than doubling Universal's annual revenues in just three years created a nearly irresistible temptation for them.

CHAPTER 22
Don't Cry

A number of our larger competitors in the security industry had expressed a varying degree of interest in acquiring Universal Protection back in the days when the company's revenues were still stuck at that $12 million plateau. By doubling its revenues in just three years, however, the interest in the company as a target of acquisition had increased correspondingly.

The situation wasn't entirely unexpected. A capitalistic Darwinism.

If anything, I think I saw the increased interest as an external validation of the improvements I had made in the company since my arrival. But I certainly wasn't surprised by the development and I wasn't caught off guard, either. My entire motivation in leaving BFI and coming to Universal had been to create a situation in which I could participate directly in the fruits of my labor and initiative through some sort of equity-sharing relationship. So, as a part of the compensation package I had negotiated with the company before coming aboard, I had demanded the inclusion of a provision that provided me with a performance-based bonus that came in the form of a certain limited ownership participation in the company. For lack of a more exact explanation, it awarded me what I referred to as a sort of "phantom equity" in the company that would guarantee me a percentage of the payout if the owners decided to sell. Fortunately for him, Brian had seen the importance of this contractual provision and then decided to negotiate a similar arrangement into his own contract. If the owners sold Universal, he stood to walk away with a sizable cash payout.

So, both Brian and I were as well positioned as we ever could've possibly been when the owners came to us and announced that they had received an offer to buy Universal Protection and they were thinking so seriously about taking it, that the buyout was almost definitely a done deal. And by that, I assumed that they had already committed to the sale and were each off deciding what automotive upgrade they were going to make in their lives with whatever up-front cash they were going to be getting from the deal.

After revealing the portrait of me that I have set out in these pages, it should come as no great surprise to anyone that I am not by nature an over-emotive sort of person. My poker-face reserve is particularly evident in the way that I handle business, where I've learned that deviating from a cold and reasoned approach is almost always a serious mistake and that one should never tip their hand to anyone. So, suffice it to say that I kept my real reaction to this bit of news to myself—and my cards close to my vest.

Brian was initially excited by the prospect of the sale when we first learned of it. His "phantom equity" was going to return him seven figures in cash and for a guy who had started his career with Universal as a security guard and then worked his way up, that sort of payout seemed like a nice cap on his career. I, however, felt his positive reaction might have betrayed his lack of a complete understanding of the situation.

I felt it was incumbent upon me to explain to him that any buyer for Universal Protection would, of course, demand that the upper tier of management enter into a non-complete clause so as to prevent them from taking their talents, knowledge, and client connections down the street and essentially re-opening the business. That would mean that Brian would be barred from working in the security industry for a significant amount of time, and so I thought that the sale of the company would really only mean one thing for him: the end of his career. And despite the generous cash payout—which I didn't think would go nearly as far as he first thought it might—I couldn't see anything in the deal that would adequately compensate him for essentially losing twenty-four years in the security business.

Furthermore, although I didn't tell Brian this at the time, I wasn't sure just how easily the skills that he'd honed over all of those years in security would translate and transfer to another industry. From my position, he was "the man" when it came to the security business, but I couldn't necessarily see him migrating and succeeding in the industrial uniform or waste management sectors. Or any other sector, for that matter.

At the end of our meeting with the owners about this potential sale, I left very quiet and contemplative. Brian left noticeably upset.

The really lousy thing about all of this was the timing of their private announcement. The owners had broken the news of this supposedly impending deal just before Christmas. Somehow, all of the chaos of the season just intensified the craziness that had been created by the announcement and all of the associated negatives and the dire picture for the future seemed all the more unsettling in the glow of holiday lights.

There was an annual holiday tradition at Universal Protection that the last Saturday before Christmas was reserved for a company-wide holiday party. The two owners would reserve a room at Club 33 at Disneyland for a dinner. The event was always a big deal and a nice night for the employees. Except for that particular holiday party.

The folks at Disneyland call it "The happiest place on earth," but I promise they wouldn't have dared to call it that if they'd attended the Universal Protection Christmas party that year.

All of the employees had enjoyed their day at the park and their night at Club 33, but none of them knew what the owners and Brian and I now knew. None of them had a clue about the pending sale of the company. So, all of these people were caught up in the holiday spirit, without realizing that they were potentially all on the perilous edge of unemployment.

We were all gathered together after dinner and it came time for one of the owners to get up and address the employees like they did every year. But this time, however, he realized that the occasion likely marked the very last time that he would ever be gathered together with these people, most of whom he'd spent an entire career with.

He rose from his seat and walked up to front of the room, but instead of a smile on his face, he looked like he had just received the worst news of his life. There were tears welling in his reddened eyes. He sniffled and stammered and started, "I'm so glad we're all together tonight. I just want to thank you all for all of your hard work—"

And that was it. That was all the guy could bring himself to say. He was just too emotional to get anything else out.

Everyone in the room looked at one another. "What's going on?"

The other partner got up and gave the annual speech a try, but that didn't go any better. Suddenly, all of the employees in the room were more concerned than curious. "What's wrong with everyone?"

Brian decided that it was up to him to show the company's stiff-upper-lip and to deliver a proper year-end Christmas speech. He bravely got up to speak, but he was the worst of them all. The guy's got a heart of gold, but it was just shattered that night at the prospect of losing the only career that he'd ever known—and the friends and people that he'd shared that with over the course of twenty-four years. Brian tried his best—and I give him all the credit in the world for even attempting to tackle what was just an incredibly emotional situation—but he simply couldn't bring himself to do it. There was no way for him to address the people that he'd worked with for so long, not knowing what he knew.

That left just me.

As I've said, I am not a guy to wear his emotions on his sleeve. And, in fairness, I had only been with Universal Protection for three years or so, and I hadn't had the opportunity to build a real attachment to the place; certainly, not the way that Brian and the owners had.

I got up and rather than being emotionally overcome, I felt that I wanted to tell everybody about the amazing year we had enjoyed. I outlined all of the many successes that the company had experienced and I thanked each and every one of them for their commitment to our shared vision. I wrapped up my comments with an inspiring speech about how optimistic I was that the coming year would far exceed what we'd already accomplished and that the best times were most definitely still in front of us all.

Good night. Merry Christmas.

None of the employees knew what to make of what had just happened before their eyes. The owners and the president had inexplicably become emotional basket cases, but The New Guy was still pumped up about how the company was going to realize accelerated gains in the coming year. It was clear that the contrasts in our holiday presentation had deeply confused (and disturbed) them all. One by one, everyone filed out of the club, shaking their heads, trying to make sense of what had just happened, completely confused. Except for Brian, who left emotionally exhausted.

I didn't leave at all. I went into the bar for a drink (or two.)

I was just finishing up when I was surprised to be joined by the owners, who came in and took seats beside me at the bar. One of them clapped me on the back and said, "Well, it's been a helluva run, hasn't it?"

I appreciated what I knew he was trying to do, but I wasn't in the mood for expressions that were meant to be more placating than meaningful. I shook my head. "The run isn't over. We're just getting started."

The owners were quick to make it clear that there wasn't room for a conversation on the subject. "Well, we've been at this a long, long time and I think it's just … it's time to sell."

There had been something on my mind since the owners had first broken the news to Brian and me and this seemed like the perfect opportunity to share it with them. "You know, you brought me in to grow your company and that's exactly what I've done. In fact, I've over-delivered and exceeded your expectations. But if I had known that you were bringing me in not for the long haul, but just to pump up the value and sell it off just three years after I started, I don't think I ever would've left BFI for that kind of arrangement. That wasn't what we originally discussed. And not what I anticipated."

"We understand you're upset. But you're going to be fine. You're young. You've got a great education. And you'll be getting a piece of the pie yourself."

"Don't get me wrong," I said. "I'm not the one crying over any of this and I'm not going to be losing any sleep, no matter what happens. If you were to sell the business right here and right now, I would be better than fine. I would go out into the market on Monday, find another position in no time, and then do for that other company what I've just done for the two of you. So none of that worries me, but selling a business that's doubled its revenue in just three years doesn't make any sense. It's stupid."

They were clearly caught off-guard by my blunt comment. "We're getting a fair price," one of them said defensively.

"Maybe you're getting a fair price today, but you're losing sight of the future. You're each going to get a lump sum and I understand that it seems like that is all that you need to get to live out the rest of your lives, but I don't believe you've thought this through. You're going to get hit with taxes." They grimaced. "And you both manage to pull a nice lifestyle out of the business: the cars, good salaries, lots of business expenses. I don't think you've taken into consideration where you're going to be when all of that goes away."

They were silent for a minute. "We'll figure it out," one of them offered defensively, but the response lacked any real conviction.

I was at the end of my drink—and my patience. "Listen, we've doubled the company's revenues in three years. That's almost unheard of in this or any other business, and you both know that. There's no limit for the growth we could experience if we just keep moving forward. You guys are getting out way too early on what could be a billion-dollar enterprise."

They both looked at me like I had just told a bad joke. "Don't be ridiculous."

I wasn't sure what they'd found to be unreasonable. "What?"

"Billion? With a B?"

"Absolutely," I said. "I came to you from BFI. It's a seven-billion-dollar enterprise today, but the founders started with just one truck. You've got all the potential to build Universal Protection into a similar player in the security industry. This could absolutely be a billion-dollar company and I'm the man who could take it there."

They both smirked, but I knew that their reaction wasn't a real evaluation of my claim, but merely an inability to see the vision for the future like I did. "Really, you think so? A billion-dollar business?"

I shook my head. "I don't think so, I know so."

They both laughed. "Well, then it sounds like you're the one who should buy it." They laughed some more.

I didn't laugh at all, because that's exactly what I'd been thinking over before they'd joined me at the bar. "That's the first thing you've been right about all night."

Their eyes opened wide. "Are you serious?"

"Dead serious. Sell me the business. Or sell it to me and Brian." I hadn't talked the prospect over with Brian, but I was confident of my ability to talk him into the arrangement.

The readiness of my reply took them both off-guard. And I think that to some extent my warnings about a future in which the IRS would leave them with a significantly depleted sum of cash that they would have to manage (and budget) for the rest of their lives had taken some of the wide-eyed-optimism they'd once had for whatever deal had been put on the table before them.

"How would you buy it?" one of them asked.

I think they meant it as a challenge, but to me it was a clear sign that I had already cleared the first hurdle and they were seriously considering the prospect of my buying them out. I didn't quite have the how worked all the way out at that particular time, but I was certain that all of the answers they would want would come to me soon. "Just give me some time. Let me—let us—come up with something. That's all that I'm asking. Before you move forward on a sale that I promise you'll regret down the road, just give us a chance to make a presentation to you. If you don't like what we have to say, then you can move ahead with your deal any way you want, but just give us a chance." I knew that was all I needed: a chance.

But here's the thing about chances: you have to be willing to take them.

You have to do your homework and be prepared to follow up with all of the day-to-day grunt work that every dream requires to eventually be transformed into something real and operational. All of those issues of risk versus gamble, certainly apply.

But here's the thing about chances: you have to be willing to take them.

At the heart of it all, however, is … well, your heart. You have to believe in yourself and you have to possess a complete commitment to the idea of realizing your dreams. Confidence.

Ultimately, I think, that's what everything in life comes down to.

That's the determinant between who achieves their dreams and who just dreams. That's the mind-set that is necessary for anyone to realize success. Most of all you need to believe you can succeed.

And I did.

CHAPTER 23
Work Out the Details

The next morning came early.

And that was just for me.

For Brian, I think my arrival at his door was almost alarming. He had left the party the night before as an emotional zombie after struggling with the thought that the company was about to be sold out from under the employees that he sincerely cared for. I know it was just the side effects of keeping that terrible secret from his co-workers, but he answered his front door looking like he had been wrecked by something else. "What are you doing here?"

"I came to talk to you."

His hung-dog look made it clear he didn't think there was much left to discuss. "About what?"

"About buying the business."

Now, in fairness to Brian, twelve hours earlier he'd been overcome by the prospect of losing the company forever; it was understandable that it took him a moment or two to wrap his head around the situation I was proposing. "Buy the business? What business?"

"Universal," I said.

He seemed surprised. And alarmed. "We can't buy the business."

"No," I corrected. "We can't *not* buy the business." I was certain about that now.

I had spent the night—and most of the early morning, too—doing some creative crunching of the numbers in order to arrive at a creative solution that might make it all work. And while I hadn't necessarily worked out all of the details, I had definitely come to the conclusion that any company that could double its revenues in just three years was not an opportunity I was willing to surrender without a fight.

Brian, however, took some more convincing.

I completely understood. He had spent twenty-four years working for the company and there was a certain security in that— even in his executive position as president—he was reluctant to surrender that degree of certainty in his life in order to move into the volatile and uncertain arena of true ownership. And that position didn't reflect any lack of confidence in his own capabilities—or in mine.

Instead, Brian's focus was then (and always has been) solely fixed on his family. He had familial responsibilities that were paramount to him and it took me a minute or two to show him how those commitments were actually better served by my proposals than by whatever deal the owners might have been considering.

So Brian and I had a long conversation.

Eventually, however, he came around. Together, we sat down to work out a business plan that we could show to the owners. Once we got to work, we figured that the company's annual revenue had virtually doubled in just three years, increasing from $12 million to $24 million. With those kind of annual returns, the owners were looking to realize about $10.8 million if they sold Universal at that point.

My idea was to convince the owners that they were selling out early and that Universal would be worth significantly more if they stayed with Brian and me and let us grow the company as we'd been doing. Using that calculation of Universal's growth as our base, we figured that if we could continue to grow the business at a similar rate, we could substantially increase the value in a relatively short period of time.

I looked over the figures and when I saw the future of the business, I set a goal of nothing less than doubling revenues. Maybe just a little bit more. This was 1999, just a week before the new millennium. I was certain that I could double the revenues again, it was merely a question of time.

Brian thought that would take about ten years, which was a perfectly reasonable but still ambitious goal. I was certain we could do it in seven. And instead of just doubling the annual revenues, I was certain that we could hit $60 million.

If that seems like a bit of braggadocios posturing, I promise it was nothing of the sort.

The problem with most people is that they don't set goals.

The problem with most people who set goals, is that they don't assign them any real terms: Deadlines. Details.

The problem with most people who set detailed goals is that they set their sights way too low. Most people will set a goal that is solidly within their comfort zone and, in my opinion, that completely defeats the purpose. A goal that is easily attainable is little more than an aspiration.

A goal that is easily attainable is little more than an aspiration.

A goal should exist at the very outer limits separating attainable-through-extraordinary-measures and absolutely impossible. Attaining a goal should require real sacrifice and test a person down to their very core. Anything less than that experience is simply the sort of concession to personal comfort that leads to complacency and settling—two conditions that are a slow and agonizing death for any dreams you wish to bring to fulfillment.

So, with an agreed-upon goal of hitting $60 million in annual revenues and growing the company to a perspective market value of $30 million, Brian and I took our proposal and our business plan to the owners. The two of them were interested enough in what we had to say that they reserved us time in the company conference room, but they still met us with a (strategic) level of reserve.

I began by repeating my concerns. "I really think you guys are making a mistake by considering an outside offer so soon in our time together." They shrugged off the suggestion. "How are you going to maintain your lifestyles without the steady income the company provides you?"

"Oh, we'll work it out," one of them answered.

There was a defensive tone to the response that let me know that they were trying to bluff a lack of concern about the long-term ramifications of the deal they were considering, but the fact that they were still sitting in front of me was a tell that my dire warnings for their futures had gotten inside their heads and, as a result, they were more than a little interested in what I had to offer them.

I went to the white board and wrote our plan across it, spelling out our intention to continue to grow the company with a goal of $60 million by 2007. "Brian and I will do it all," I explained. "You guys can basically retire. You guys can just exit the business if you're tired of working it. We totally understand. Go travel. Enjoy your lifestyles. Brian and I will do all of the work and we will take all of the risk."

They tried to pretend their interest was casual. "Well, that all sounds good, but how do we know that you guys will stick around to see it all through? What's to say that we don't pass up this deal we got now and then a year from now, you two are gone and we're left without a deal at all?"

Skipping out on the company was not on my To-Do list. "Well, we're not going anywhere, because we're going to do this—we're going to continue to grow your company at these amazing rates—because in exchange, we're going to get an equity interest. We're going to become owners with you two."

They winced, but they didn't walk.

"When we get to $60 million in revenues," I explained. "When we hit that number—and we'll hit it by 2007—then you give us a 40 percent interest in the company—but only if we hit that number and only if we do it in that time frame. If we don't meet those conditions, then we're out."

Both of the owners recognized the win/win I was putting in front of them and they sat up in their seats, exchanging looks that I knew meant they were more than interested. They hemmed and hawed. "Well, that deal we're considering is going to drop some serious cash on us and it's hard to walk away from that. If you're going to make an offer for our company, then we'd like to get a little bit of money up front."

Unfortunately, Brian and I didn't have the cash to put down, but I was convinced we had something just as good. "Brian and I both have our equity in the company. If you went ahead with the sale, I was going to walk away with $500,000. Brian would walk away with a $1 million even. We'll both turn all of that over to you. That's a $1.5 million."

They laughed. "No, that was a $1.5 million in cash only if we went through with the sale. But you two want us to walk away from the deal and if we do that, your equity interest isn't worth anything at all."

The ball was back in our court. I didn't hesitate. I knew I was close to making my plan a reality and I wasn't going to let anything sink that deal, including the ability to put up a little bit of cash. "We need to talk to a lender. Just give us a chance to get some money together for you," I said. "Just let us get to the bank."

They smiled a different kind of smile.

Later that week, Brian and I took that same business plan to our bank and secured a loan for $1 million dollars. All of it went right back to the owners; half a million to each of them. In addition to that lump sum payment, they also got a significant increase in their "salaries."

The deal Brian and I were left with was that we had seven years to grown the company's annual revenues past $60 million. If we hit that number in the time allotted, then we wound up sharing a 40 percent interest in Universal. But if we didn't hit that number in that time, then Brian and I surrendered our phantom equity interest, forfeited any ownership interest at all, and were still on the line for the $1 million loan we'd taken out to get the owners their upfront cash.

It took us close to a year to have the lawyers work out all of the language on a complicated deal like that. There was a lot of back-and-forth and a lot of lawyers who had to dot the i's and cross the t's, but what I am proudest of is that while we waited for a final written contract, the four of us went forward with this multi-million-dollar deal, all on the guarantee of nothing more than a handshake.

They were just handshakes, but we all honored that obligation of having given our word. I think that says a lot about all of us.

In this day and age, I think it's important that people come to the bargaining table—no matter how much money may be in play—with a commitment in their heart that a deal is a deal and the honor to abide by that oath.

I understand that at this point many of you may be recalling what I've previously written about taking risks, but never gambling, but I assure you there's no contradiction there. I stand by every line that I've written and I wouldn't walk-back a word of it.

Our unique deal certainly had elements of significant risk, but nothing about it was a gamble. Not at all.

I had done my research and knew exactly what had to be done in order to satisfy the conditions we had created for ourselves. Most important of all, I was committed to making it happen. It wasn't a gamble, it was a goal.

And the final thing that's wrong with most people who set goals: they stand back and wait for them to be accomplished, like fate or fortune have some role to play in the achievement. Not me, I had set a goal and I was willing to do everything necessary to make sure that I met it.

CHAPTER 24
Just Grind

Of course, the last thing about goals … it's always a lot tougher to achieve them than you ever thought it would be.

Brian and I knew we needed to aggressively expand the business, but the problem was that there were very few resources left at our disposal to make all of that happen. As soon as our deal was made, the owners basically followed up on my invitation to step away from the business. Once in a great while, one of them would pop in to the Universal offices to chat up the people (and relatives) in the office or to catch lunch with Brian and me in order to see how we were getting along in our efforts to satisfy that goal. For the most part, however, Brian and I were on our own.

Together, we became co-CEOs, which sounds like a designation destined for conflict, but the two of us found a synergy between us that worked (almost) perfectly.

The only obstacle that we had in our path to success was a disturbing lack of capital. Most of our available credit was tied up in the million-dollar loan we'd taken to give the owners cash. Beyond that, their "salary adjustment" had created a situation in which much of the business' liquidity was being funneled right back out the door to the owners. As a result, our efforts to expand the business at that time were necessarily made on a shoestring budget.

First up was an area known to the residents of Southern California as the Inland Empire. For those not as familiar with the region, the Inland Empire would generally include the cities west of Riverside

County and in southwest San Bernardino County, but I think it would also be fair to include the eastern Los Angeles County cities in the Pomona Valley, maybe even out into the surrounding desert communities. The area was filled with prospects, but we needed a formal presence there before we could begin to make any serious entrée into the area.

We opened a branch office out in the heart of the Inland Empire. Technically it was an office, I suppose, but it would be far more accurate to describe our accommodations out there as a branch closet. The more important factor, however, was that the address opened the market up to us for the first time and we wasted no time in maximizing our presence there. In no time at all, the Inland Empire had become very successful for us.

Next on the list was San Diego.

Our newest office was just another closet, but it allowed us to make our move down south to a very fertile market. Everything down there started with a contract for just a single building. That contract led us to another, and another. Before we knew it, we had worked the entire San Diego area in the most organic fashion, adding more and more customers to our roster until we were a real presence in the area.

This was all part of the plan. I had learned that path from Aramark and BFI. Those models had provided a blueprint for my own vision and we executed on that vision systematically. There was nothing fancy to our scheme, nothing that I had pulled from course work in business school.

We made our success the old-fashioned way: We just got into the market and started to grind. And grind. And grind.

In addition to the physical presences we were establishing with all of these new branch offices, we were also finally able to build up our sales team the way that I had always envisioned. I put together my dream team, staffing it with quality people.

As a side note, I think that's one of the most important components of achieving success in almost any endeavor is being able to build a team that's capable of working together towards that success.

Far too many executives follow a hiring protocol that is focused on candidates with specific skills, backgrounds, and/or experience. I certainly understand the logic behind this approach toward hiring, but it overlooks the more important consideration, which is hiring people of personal quality, employees who can get behind the team 100 percent.

One of the most important components of achieving success in almost any endeavor is being able to build a team that's capable of working together towards that success.

Anyone can be trained to execute this specific task or that, but even the most pedigreed candidate who can't buy into the company philosophy and become a team player is a significant handicap that needs to be removed. Our hires for the sales force were all people I knew I could rely on to do everything that was asked of them.

What was asked of them initially was to contact existing customers who had buildings in these new territories that we didn't have under contract, and then build relationships. Sooner than later, we had their buildings in these new areas, too.

Step by step, we worked our plan methodically. Existing businesses. New businesses. Our client list continued to grow.

The next move was up into Northern California. And we did it in the most fantastic way.

We had previously acquired the contract for security services at the Transamerica Building in Southern California. It was an important jewel in our crown and I was able to develop a very close relationship with the building's property manager. Through that connection, we were able to secure the contract for providing security services to the Transamerica Pyramid Building in San Francisco. Forget the fact that this is unquestionably the most iconic building in all of San Francisco; the structure is arguably in the running with the Empire State Building and Willis Tower as the most iconic building in all of the United States.

When anyone thinks of San Francisco, this is the building they see in their mind's eye. And we were protecting it!

This was a monumental achievement for a company that was just then beginning its expansion into the region, and that presence opened a lot of doors to us that I'm confident would've otherwise remained shut. And locked.

At the same time, while our company was servicing these really important buildings, our liquidity problems were putting considerable restraints on our ability to maximize this opportunity. For example, we had just signed the contract on the Transamerica Pyramid and staffed it out, when we realized that simply getting the necessary uniforms from our offices in Southern California up to the Bay Area would have been prohibitively expensive for us.

So, given our lack of cash, I decided that the most cost-effective means of getting the uniforms to our newest location was to throw them all in the back of my old Ford Explorer and drive them up there myself. (The owners were all driving Mercedes and Jaguars, but I was the co-CEO and still driving a beat-up Explorer. In fact, the Explorer was such a beater that I only got to the outskirts of Bakersfield on my way north with a cargo of uniforms before the damn thing broke down.)

There I was, a co-CEO of this multi-million-dollar company, stranded on the highway with an Explorer that couldn't roll another mile. In the end, I had to rent a van just to get the uniforms up to San Francisco in time to open the building.

After that, this uniform run became a weekly routine for me. I would drive back up to San Francisco with a fresh load of uniforms, drop them off, and then head back to Southern California. I made that same circuitous uniform delivery trip every week for more than a year.

When I was in Northern California, I couldn't even afford to stay in San Francisco, where the hotel rooms were all $300 on up. Instead, I'd drive over the bridge to Oakland and find something that we could manage on our budget at the time; if times were good, that was maybe a Holiday Inn; if times were tough, it was some sketchy motel that wouldn't cost me more than $100 a night.

I remember on one of these northern excursions, I had stopped for dinner at a Denny's adjacent my motel parking lot at the end of a very long day. It was late, after 10:00 p.m. I was sitting at the counter and had just finished whatever microwaved entree had been on the plate when I came to an unexpected realization.

The waitress seemed more tired than I was and she kind of sighed when I asked, "Do you have anything special for dessert?"

"Ice cream. We have ice cream."

"I'll have that."

She set a bowl of ice cream in front of me and asked, "Is that special enough for you?"

I smiled. "I just remembered, it's my thirtieth birthday today."

Without saying a word or missing a beat, she pulled a matchbook from her apron pocket, struck a light, and then stuck it (and her fingers) straight into my ice cream. "Happy Birthday."

Absolutely none of that is a complaint.

I think back on all of those trips—maybe not the one on which I wound up stranded on the side of the road in Bakersfield—but all of the other trips, I remember fondly as the building blocks that we were putting in place to build our business into something bigger. And as our business continues to grow, I like to think back on those days as a way to keep grounded.

Too many people frame their business goals around what are essentially the end results—the first-class travel and admittedly luxurious accommodations—and they fail to understand the very personal sacrifices that are often necessary to ascend to that status in the first place.

It's a serious mistake to overlook that component. And those who aren't willing to roll up their sleeves and load the uniforms into their busted down SUV are unlikely to ever get the point of success that they feel should be handed to them.

The fact of the matter is that Brian and I were grinding. Just grinding. And I loved every minute of it. What I loved most of all, however, was that we were realizing tangible results from all of those considerable efforts.

When we first started, Brian and I would drive through Los Angeles and look at all of the skyscrapers. I'd point out the ones that we were going to add to our client roster and Brian would tell me why that would be impossible for us to get under contract for one reason or another. "They're locked in a contract with this company." "They're only going with a certain kinda company."

But I've never been one to accept any limitations on my dreams. I went door-to-door to each and every one of those "impossible" buildings and introduced myself, explaining what Universal could do for them that other security companies just couldn't. I met with the property managers, developed relationships, and struck up friendships. Piece by piece.

Not only did we get the Transamerica Building in Los Angeles and the Transamerica Pyramid in San Francisco, but we had all of those buildings that we'd dreamt about throughout Century City. We topped it all off by signing up the Library Tower, the tallest building west of the Mississippi at seventy-five stories.

We were grinding and growing and the future was bright. And then something happened.

Something that changed our company and our industry forever. Something that changed me. That changed everyone. And everything.

CHAPTER 25
9/11

I am a tough man. That's not me bragging, that's just an undeniable statement of fact.

Since the time I was a kid, I was raised and trained for just one thing: to hit the toughest guys on the other team so hard and so often that, eventually, over the course of the game, they weren't so tough anymore. And I was damn good at it, too.

I am a tough guy and tough guys don't cry.

But that day was different.

I hardly ever sleep, so I was already up when my phone rang. It was about six in the morning. On the other end of the line was a good friend of mine who ran one of our largest accounts. He was a client, but he was something more to me, too. Another mentor who had taken me under his wing and provided some much needed (and appreciated) guidance.

His early morning phone call was certainly unusual, but because we were such good friends I didn't think anything more of it than that. "What are you doing?" he asked.

"I just got out of the shower and I'm—"

"Turn on the TV."

I didn't understand. "The TV?"

"Turn on the TV." I still didn't understand the command, but there was something in the tone of his voice that compelled me to comply.

I flipped on my television. The black screen came to life … and I saw the second plane slam into the Twin Towers.

"What do we do?" my friend asked.

I didn't even stop to think. "We've got to evacuate. Now."

"What buildings?"

"All of them," I said.

I was living in Mission Viejo, in Orange County, California, at the time and I started driving north for Los Angeles. The news reports on the radio as I drove along were terrifying. At the time, no one knew how many planes had been hijacked and so every jetliner in the sky was seen as a potential threat. I drove into LA and made sure that all of our buildings were evacuated and locked down.

Then I hustled over to Century City and did the same thing there.

Our clients were understandably panicked, asking us when they would be able to reopen and what they should be doing in the meantime. We didn't know. Nobody knew anything in those terrible times.

And then I got a call from the property manager for the Transamerica Pyramid in San Francisco. She had five words for me. "We need you up here." Of course, by this time, all commercial air traffic had been grounded, so there were no flights to get me there in a hurry.

Instead, I took to the highway and made the usual six-hour drive in just over four. I parked outside the Transamerica Pyramid and was rushing to get inside, when I suddenly stopped in my tracks.

The silence.

I had been a regular visitor to the city so many times over the course of my life, but I had never heard it so damn silent. There wasn't a plane in the sky. Minimal traffic on the roads. Just a handful of people on the street.

Silence.

It was as if the entire city had shut down in a solemn observation of the tragedy that had just befallen our nation. In just one day, everything had changed.

I am a tough guy. As tough as they come.

And I am not afraid or ashamed to tell you that I cried that day.

It was as if the entire city had shut down in a solemn observation of the tragedy that had just befallen our nation.

CHAPTER 26
Rise to the Occasion

The events of 9/11 were seismic. Before that terrible day, it would have been difficult for (almost) anyone to have foreseen those tragic events unfolding the way that they did. And that may explain why none of our competitors had any preparations for such a situation.

While they floundered in their own indecisions, I knew it was critical that we take charge of the situation. We needed to take steps to not only ensure our clients' buildings protection, but also to create a situational environment of confidence around the properties that we protected.

At that time, we represented a couple of malls and a handful of retail centers, but probably 90 percent of our business was with commercial office buildings, so our clientele felt particularly vulnerable in those dark days in the immediate aftermath of the attack.

We went to work (overtime) to address those special needs. We hired and assigned extra guards to every property and within twenty-four to thirty-six hours after the attacks, we not only had every one of our buildings open for business, but we also had instituted all of the previously underutilized security protocols that are now commonly used in most public buildings and venues: bag checks, car scans in parking garages, heightened public interface from our security officers.

It was an amazing process, in just a little over twenty-four hours, we had completely revamped our approach to security. And, in doing so, we learned that we were suddenly at the forefront of our industry in this regard.

It wasn't just the other midsized companies like us that we were eclipsing, it was all of the biggest players on the field, as well. Like everyone else in the country, the companies that were considered the security giants at the time had been caught completely off guard by those terrible events and they could not demonstrate an ability to adapt and respond in a meaningful fashion, certainly not the same way that we had done for our customers.

People began to take notice of us. Our phones began to ring, not just with new customers—although there were plenty of those—but from people who were overwhelmed by what had happened and the monumental implications moving forward. Still stunned by the tragedy, people were uncertain about what they needed to do to protect themselves and their property, and they turned to us for guidance.

What I realized in the aftermath was that the damage done to our nation by these terrorist attacks was not limited to the lives so tragically taken or the substantial property damage that had been created. Instead, there was an emotional wound that had been opened up across the country, a savage blow to our collective psyche, and an injury that needed to be triaged and treated by someone.

As part of our measures to provide an adequate response to our existing customers, I had created (almost overnight) a presentation that outlined what Universal Protection was doing to step-up the level of security that we would be delivering moving forward and what the properties themselves could do to assist in those efforts and to provide an environment that offered their tenants and guests some badly needed confidence in the building's overall safety in the event of any foreseeable hostile activity.

We reached out and involved the Federal Bureau of Investigations and brought in their representatives. We worked with Los Angeles County Police Department and Orange County Sheriff Department. We brought in the best of the best and together we formulated a cohesive policy and protocol for security moving forward into what had clearly become a brand-new age.

We reviewed the indicators of terrorist activity that everyone now needed to be alert to, preparedness and evacuation procedures, and general steps that could be taken to improve their building's overall security. We talked about what had gone wrong in New York and what they could do to avoid making similar mistakes. We discussed absolutely everything that was necessary to harden the security around their buildings.

We were, for all intents and purposes, the only company to take these measures—and certainly the only firm to offer programs that were even remotely on this level. Once we got started, there were a few weak imitators, but their inadequacies were quickly discerned and they dropped right back out of the running.

Our presentations, however, were a huge success. Our customers really responded to them. And then we began to get requests from property managers at buildings we did not have under contract who were in need of this information but were unable to find it anywhere else.

We rented ballrooms and invited guests. The presentation cost us about $30,000 (all in) but by the time we were done, the investment had provided results and returns that we never could have anticipated.

And then in no time, we were fielding requests from property managers from other buildings who wanted to attend our sessions because their current security service providers weren't up to speed and were unable to address their very real concerns about the future. And after each session, these same property managers were lining up for the opportunity to give us their business cards and ask us for the opportunity to sit down and talk about the prospects of working together in the future.

The program was so popular that I wound up developing a two-hour PowerPoint presentation with the input from the FBI and various major police departments and then taking the show on the road. I delivered the presentation all over California, and then throughout the Southwest, and then eventually across the country. For the best part of a year, I gave the presentation almost daily. I talked and answered questions until I had lost my voice and couldn't talk anymore—literally. For more than a year, I travelled regularly, spreading the information that we had collected and, with it, the name and reputation of Universal Protection.

> **At a moment of national vulnerability, when everyone else was overwhelmed and disorganized, we had stepped up and acted decisively and confidently. What we needed to learn, we took to the best experts available and sought out the answers we needed.**

At a moment of national vulnerability, when everyone else was overwhelmed and disorganized, we had stepped up and acted decisively and confidently. What we needed to learn, we took to the best experts available and sought out the answers we needed. And we concentrated not on selfishly taking advantage of the situation, but on providing a service to the community that was genuine and of considerable worth.

By taking these steps, we were able to make dramatic inroads into both previously untapped markets and into the customer base of our competitors. The results for our business were incredible and it ushered us into a time of growth that even we never could have imagined or anticipated.

CHAPTER 27
Prepare for Success

As a result of this incredible period of growth, we were able to absolutely shatter the goals that we had previously set for ourselves within the deal we had structured with the owners.

In just two years—by the end of 2002—we had taken the business from $24 million to $48 million. While it had previously taken us three years to double the revenue, we'd managed to accomplish that same staggering achievement in almost half of the time.

The thing about that explosive growth was that it attracted attention and fed additional expansion. The more that property managers heard about what we were doing to revolutionize the delivery of customer-based security services, the more they wanted to be a part of that movement as well. Our sales department was still doing an incredible job, but now our phones were ringing off the hook with property managers beginning the call with, "We'd like to talk to you about security."

We continued acquiring new customers at that pace of expansion and by 2004—three years ahead of the ambitious goal we had set for ourselves, the company's annual revenues were in excess of $60 million.

We had accomplished everything we'd set out after in half the time we'd allowed ourselves. The irony was that this created some serious difficulties for us with our partners.

When we hit that $60 million figure, our owners were ecstatic. "That's great! The company is now worth more than twice what we were originally planning to sell it for. We're glad we listened to you back then, but now it's definitely time to sell."

> **Success. I had prepared for it and worked for it and, I have to tell you, it was every bit as sweet as I'd always thought it would be.**

Brian and I couldn't believe what they were telling us. We had worked so hard, sacrificed so much, and now that we were only approaching the threshold of the true potential of the company, the two guys who hadn't had any involvement in that growth wanted to sell it out from under us.

Brian and I insisted, "No, our deal was that we got to develop the company until 2007. The $60 million was the qualifier for us to assume a 40 percent equity interest in the company, but the term of the deal was for seven years."

For a deal that had been reduced to writing by lawyers but was still largely governed by handshakes, relations became momentarily tense. Fortunately (for everyone), we were again able to salvage the deal. Brian and I had done what everyone else had said was impossible. We had made our goal. And for the first time in my life ... I had ownership interest.

Success.

I had prepared for it and worked for it and, I have to tell you, it was every bit as sweet as I'd always thought it would be.

CHAPTER 28
Find A Way

My partner and I had achieved far greater success than anyone could have ever hoped for, but that wasn't enough to keep our original partners satisfied. In fact, the significant increase in value that we had brought to Universal only seemed to confirm their instinctive sense that they had lucked into a very profitable situation and they were not shy about taking full advantage of that.

Don't get me wrong, I was mindful of and gracious for the opportunity that they had given Brian and me by accepting our original offer. I was equally aware, however, that the financial rewards they had reaped as a result of our efforts to grow their company were far more than they ever could have realized if they had refused our offer and proceeded to sell the business as they had first intended.

Still, I never for a moment thought there was anything personal about the position they assumed afterward. I always understood that they were both shrewd businessmen who simply realized that the unexpected growth of their company under my direction had significantly improved their bargaining position and they were intent on using that to secure the best possible deal for themselves. Just business.

Nevertheless, the phenomenal success that Brian and I had achieved came to us as a double-edged sword, and the original partners used the sharpest side to get us to further sweeten a deal that was already plenty sugary. Despite the unbelievable results that we had achieved in growing the company and the limitless potential that I had recognized and begun to develop, the original owners continued to use the threat of selling the company out from beneath us until we negotiated another sizable "salary" increase.

Of course, I knew that ultimately their decision to sell Universal to anyone but Brian and me would have cost them money in the long run. I know they knew that, too. Still, they were both willing to bet that I was so convinced in the potential of the company and my own vision for its future that I would pay a premium to preserve them both. They were absolutely right.

We had no choice but to give in to what I always suspected was their bluff. So, Brian and I went back to the banks and borrowed another $5 million to keep them from selling and in exchange for us receiving another 10 percent in equity. That was a steep price to pay, but the equity we received balanced the scales for the first time in our working relationship. Brian and I were now 50/50 owners in the company.

At this point, however, Universal was no longer just some little mom-and-pop security operation tucked away in a corner of Southern California. By the time that the 2007 deadline had come around, we were a rising star in the industry, with offices throughout all of California and outpost offices in the new territories of Arizona and Colorado. Our annual revenues had just gone north of $150 million.

Remarkably, all of that incredible growth had been 100 percent organic. There were no acquisitions involved, just good ol' fashioned, nose-to-grindstone hard work by the best sales team in the business. And while those achievements were all something to be proud of, I was keenly aware that it was not going to be enough to get our company where I knew it could be—and, more importantly, where

STEVE JONES

I knew it had to be in order to survive in a tightening market filled with larger, predatory competitors.

The organic growth was great, but I knew that there were inherent limitations to the progress we could make and only so much more that we could do if we continued along that same path.

That wasn't indicative of any shortcomings on behalf of our sales team. To the contrary, I don't think there can be any question but that they consistently demonstrated that they were (and are) the very best in this business. No, the limitations were all simply a matter of mathematics.

There were only so many potential customers in the regions that we could practically serve. That meant that if we were going to have a chance of keeping up our tremendous growth rate, we were going to have to try something different. Something bold.

Our first acquisition was in 2007. Ligouri and Associates was a relatively small, but highly respected company based in San Francisco. At the time, Universal was probably earning annual revenues in the neighborhood of $150 million. Ligouri and Associates was probably earning annual revenues of somewhere around $12 million.

That year, Lou Ligouri and I were brought together as two of the "little" guys in labor negotiations with the union that was dominated by two or three of the billion-dollar companies in the industry. None of those real heavy-hitters wanted to treat guys like Lou or me as if we had any significance to the industry and, therefore, anything to say in the negotiations. They were national giants who wanted to control everything, and they were quick to write us both off as just two little California companies.

(Free piece of advice: never dismiss or act contemptuously toward anyone you come in contact with. You never know, the guy

151

you won't talk to today might just dominate the industry in a couple of years. Live by that.)

So, Lou and I ended up as being the spokespeople for the "little" guys in these labor negotiations. We had similar interests and we fought hard to protect them where the big companies would have otherwise just rolled right over all of us. In the course of that struggle, Lou and I became friends.

(More free advice: personal relationships are everything in business and life.)

Lou and I were sitting one afternoon having some lunch, discussing the frustrating position of having to negotiate with the labor union and the big companies that should've been protecting our interests, when I happened to ask him, "What are your long-term plans?"

Personal relation-ships are everything in business and life. His answer surprised me. Before he had ever entered the security industry, Lou had completed and retired from a distinguished career with the San Francisco Police Department. With the changing market and the ongoing labor negotiations, however, he confessed to me that he was growing tired of the daily struggle and was thinking seriously of selling his business.

I was intrigued and told him so. There was only one problem: money.

Brian and I had just borrowed a bunch of it to pay off the original owners (again) and I wasn't certain just how we would get our hands on more. Of course, I wasn't about to let a little detail like a lack of money stop me from taking advantage of what I recognized was a great opportunity for the company. Over a couple more lunches and a dinner or two, I managed to convince Lou that if he really wanted to sell his business, then Universal was the right party to buy it from him. We shook hands on the deal. Of course, I knew that getting Lou's handshake was going to be the easiest part of the acquisition. The next step was going to be much, much harder.

I flew back home and walked into Brian's office to share with him what I hoped (but doubted) he might receive as good news.

"Are you crazy?" My partner looked at me like I'd grown another head.

The nice thing about my relationship with Brian, the thing that made him such a perfect partner for me, was that no matter how exasperated his "Are you out of your mind?" might have sounded, his exclamations were almost always translated as, "I trust you, but convince me."

We sat and talked things over for a while and I managed to do just that. I explained to him that with the acquisition of Ligouri and Associates, Universal would instantly grow and that type of growth would significantly alter our presence in the state.

Eventually, Brian signed on. This was a victory for sure, but hardly the only battle I was going to have to fight.

The next step in the process was going to the original partners and somehow convincing them to acquiesce to this acquisition, when all along they had repeatedly threatened to sell Universal themselves. The conversation was a tricky one. Let's just say that there was only one thing that would convince them. I believe that the phrase they used was, "Well, maybe offer us a little candy to do this." "A little candy" meant another million dollars or two.

With all of that work (and money) to convince the original partners, I was still only halfway to my goal of acquiring Lou's company. I still needed to get the purchase money to make the actual deal go through.

I did my due diligence and then went to the banks and said, "Here's the business we want to buy. Here's what we're going to get out of it in terms of operational synergies and additional revenue. I'd like to borrow against some of that."

Cue the cricket noises. Just nothing. The banks looked at me exactly like Brian had … and the original owners had … like I was absolutely out of my mind for wanting to take on this acquisition.

The best I could do was to find a lender who would offer us about half of the total sum that I needed to buy the company.

At this point, I think most people in my position would have just thrown up their hands and concluded that the deal wasn't meant to be, accepted defeat, and agreed that it just wasn't the right time to start acquiring companies. I'm not most people.

I jumped on a Southwest flight and flew up to San Francisco to talk to Lou and his wife, Chris, directly. They were lovely people and over the course of the many discussions that followed, we all became very close friends. In the end, I was able to convince them to accept the amount I knew I could secure from the banks as a down payment, with the remaining 50 percent to be paid out over the following five years.

Looking back on it now, it's odd that I never worried about those arrangements. I never worried that I was taking my friends' company with the guarantee that I would pay them half its value over time without any certainty of where that payment would be coming from. When I shook Lou and Chris's hands on that deal, I just *knew* that I was going to make it all work out.

And it did. Perfectly.

Both Lou and Chris came to work for our organization. Some of their key employees came with them, too.

The acquisition helped us double our presence in San Francisco, offered us more resources, and gave us an office in Napa Valley, where they had been headquartered.

Of course, I made absolutely certain that we paid off every dime that we owed them. The acquisition turned out to be a fantastic deal for all of us. The Ligouris received an absolute premium for their company and we added the first acquisition to our still-growing business.

What I treasure most about that transaction, however, isn't necessarily the business advantages that we gained, but rather the wonderful friendship I forged with the Ligouris.

Tragically, Lou passed away shortly after our transaction, but Chris remains a close friend to this day. Lou's loss is still felt by all who knew him.

CHAPTER 29
Follow Your Gut

By 2008, the success and amazing growth that Universal had experienced had not gone unnoticed within the industry. And beyond.

One day I got an unexpected call from an investment banker who informed me that he represented a very big company from India that had heard about what our company had done, the remarkable growth that we had demonstrated. They loved us. They wanted to buy us. The offer was certainly something to consider.

Now, every year there is a major security convention for those of us within the industry. In 2008, the location was Atlanta and this would've been a perfect place to meet with that interested party—except that I had no plans to attend that year.

I had other things on my mind. Actually, the choice to skip the convention wasn't exactly all mine. My wife was due to give birth to our second son and she had made it very clear that there was *noooo* way I was leaving her alone to attend a conference in Hot-lanta. I'm smarter than to have argued the point.

Brian, however, was intrigued by the offer from India and he flew to Atlanta without me to meet with the investment banker and his interested clients. Apparently, they all had a meeting that included an offer to buy the company and Brian liked what he heard. A lot.

He liked what he heard so much that he and the banker and the representatives from India all got on a plane and flew out to Los Angeles to talk with me personally. When they landed, I got a phone

157

call from Brian and he said, "Hey, the guys from India are here in Newport Beach. They want to meet you. And I really want you to hear what they have to say, because I think you're going to like it as much as I do."

I wasn't exactly free to talk, however, so I told him, "I've got to call you back because I am literally in the delivery room right now."

My son was born. Mother and child were doing great. (Thank God.)

My phone rang again and Brian seemed less patient, "They're waiting."

Now, my wife was understandably exhausted from her ordeal and was falling in and out of sleep. My newborn son had been taken to the maternity ward where they do all of the weighing and measuring and check-up procedures that they do to babies.

I looked at my watch. It was around noon and it struck me that, with mother and child both otherwise occupied, I might have a very small window of opportunity to meet with the potential buyers who were just ten minutes down the street.

I ducked out of the hospital, hopped in my car, and sped down to where they were all waiting. Brian introduced me to the banker and the folks from India. We sat down and they told us how much they admired Universal and how interested they were in acquiring the company as their entry into the market in the United States.

We started talking. It turned out that Brian was right, I did like what they had to say. I liked it so much that I sat and listened. And listened. And listened.

I happen to be a man who has a true appreciation for a very well-made watch, but it doesn't matter what's on your wrist when it tells you that you've been away from your wife in the hospital for six hours.

Now, I already knew that I was in trouble when I got back to the hospital, but I figured that I could stay just a little while longer and still make it back in time to smooth things out with her.

Another check of my watch. 7:00 p.m. *Soooooooo* much trouble.

A check of my watch. Nine. At this point, I was just glad that when I finally got back to my wife I would already be at the hospital.

Eventually, the meeting came to an end and when I finally made it back to my wife's hospital room, the only thing that kept me out of the Intensive Care Unit was that I fully explained just how generous the deal was. I set out everything we would stand to gain, and not just in a business sense. I let her know everything that the deal would mean to us as a (newly expanded) family.

Fortunately, she was persuaded and ultimately forgave me—and, by that, I mean that she gave me the opportunity to make it up to her.

The next step forward was a meeting in New York. Brian and I flew out with our lawyer, Larry Braun. There was no doubt that the deal on the table was a very generous one, but the closer we came to closing on the offered sale, the more Brian and I began to have misgivings. I think we realized that we still owed the original partners a balloon payment on the company. Then there was the other indebtedness.

And, quite frankly, we had both just spent so much time and effort—invested so much of ourselves—into building Universal up to what it had become that there was something that just didn't sit right with us about selling the company. None of that changed the fact that selling Universal was certainly a smart business move to make, but the prospect just broke my heart to think of the finality of it all.

When it came down to it, Universal was *ours* and I didn't want to see it go to anyone else. Not at any price.

Larry must have sensed our unease. He said, "If this is all just about money, then I can get you money. I will help you find the money you need."

I don't think I need to add that at this particular time in the global economy, there weren't a lot of institutions that were left unscathed by the growing crisis in banking and even fewer that were making capital available to borrowers like us. Everything was crumbling and going straight to hell. And I mean everything.

At the time, we had lines of credit with two banks, Comerica Bank and Guarantee Bank.

While all of this was going on, we got a call early one Friday afternoon from our banker at Comerica, who told us that Guarantee was going under. "Guarantee is going to be taken over by regulators. They're going to announce it on Monday, but we wanted you to hear about it now because your line of credit will be frozen and you won't be able to draw on it any longer." We'd been feeling the squeeze of limited credit all along, so the news of the collapse of one of our two banks was alarming, to say the least.

Crisis time. It was doubtful whether we could have continued without the available credit and we needed to arrive at some emergency solution.

After a few gut-wrenching hours, our CFO came up with the idea to draw down on both of our existing accounts that afternoon and then to invest what we'd just taken out into a third bank account, from which we could continue to pay our ongoing business expenses. We called this "Hail Mary" play and put it into action. We ultimately managed to beat the clock with absolutely no time left on the play clock.

So, at this particular point, it wouldn't have been an overstatement to have said that the company's finances were in a difficult position. We had just maxed out the only lines of credit that we could get. We still owed money on the debt we'd run up to pay off the partners. And there was still more money due to our original partners. Lots of debt.

To make these matters even worse, the banking world was crumbling all around us and everything in the business media was suggesting that things were only going to get worse. Lenders were more than just tight.

When we arrived in New York, we offered our sincere apologies to the group from India and jetted back to California. Universal was not for sale.

My point in all of this is that there was a lot of business sense in selling Universal and then using those funds as a means to get out from under a mountain of debt. I knew that, but I was still interested in what Larry had said to us. "Don't do this deal with the party from India if you don't want to do it. If your only motivation is money, then don't do the deal. I will help you find the money that you need."

I looked at Brian and he looked at me. When we arrived in New York, we offered our sincere apologies to the group from India and jetted back to California. Universal was not for sale.

CHAPTER 30
Find A Solution

Several days after Brian and I put an end to the sale with the guys from India, I received another call. This time the people on the other end of the line were from Caltius Partners, a mezzanine finance group. For the uninitiated, a mezzanine group typically offers good-sized companies like Universal Protection a high-dollar loan, but at high interest rates. I knew from the start that it might not be an ideal solution to our issues, but it was a solution—and we needed one of those.

I set up a meeting with the people from Caltius and we talked things over. They loved our company, our story, and the vision we had for growing it further. I told them all about the Ligouri acquisition.

And then I sold them on my background at BFI and my familiarity with their acquisitions process. I told them that while I was with the company, they had made hundreds of acquisitions to really grow the company and I had been on the ground in my region actively integrating those companies. My plan for Universal Protection was to follow that same proven format of successive acquisitions as a means of growing our own company.

I never had any doubt about our ability to make good on my bold assertions

If in that discussion I in any way oversold the exact extent of my expertise in large-scale, multiple corporate acquisitions, then I promise that I never had any doubt about our ability to make good on my bold assertions, nevertheless.

The people from Caltius left our conversation, made whatever calculations that they needed to assess our proposal, and then they came back to us with some very good news. They had been impressed with what we had done with Universal Protection and our vision for the future, so impressed that they found it was a future that they very much wanted to be a part of. They told us that they would be willing to loan us all of the money that we needed to position the business exactly where we thought it should be.

That was *a lot*. They offered to loan us the money we needed to buy out the original partners and to take care of all of the associated financial obligations, so that we would own the company outright. And they offered to loan us all the money that we might conceivably need so that we could begin to make acquisitions in accordance with the aggressive philosophy I wanted to put in play in order to grow the business to the level of greatness I knew it was capable of achieving. So, just like that, all of our problems were solved.

All of our problems were solved … but at a steep, steep price. There was no doubt that Caltius Partners was the solution to the financial dilemmas we were working our way through, but I certainly don't want to create the impression that they did us any favors. We were borrowing all of that money at 14 percent interest, with an additional 5 percent due at the end of the loan, for a grand total of 19 percent interest, *plus* 3 percent warrants or equity interest in the business itself. So, nothing about it came as a favor. No, it was just business.

From a "just business" standpoint, however, the cash infusion from Caltius Partners was a significant lifeline because it took care of the problems that we had been experiencing and positioned us to take the next steps that I knew we needed to take in order to grow the business.

Brian, however, had his doubts. I couldn't blame him for harboring concerns about what was an admittedly questionable strategic step. I was proposing borrowing millions (and millions) of dollars at 19 percent interest. That was essentially like running our business on a Discover card. There was no doubt that it was a risky move. Risky, however, was exactly what we needed.

The interest rate on the borrowed money was so high that if we'd favored caution and relied solely on the sort of steady organic growth we were experiencing, there was no way that we could have made the arrangement work out for us. No, in order to stay ahead of that killer interest rate, we had to grow the business at an even steeper rate. And that required—risk.

At this point, however, Brian had had his fill of risk. Understandably, he wanted me to consider whether it was time to accept the limitations that so many others had always tried to put upon us and finally sell the company, clear the debts, and cash in on the success that we had amassed up to that point.

I appreciated the strength of his argument, of course, but my vision was even stronger. Brian eventually decided to trust me "one more time" and we took the offered money from Caltius. With those funds, we paid off the original owners once and for all, and that meant that the company was entirely ours. We now made all of the decisions and there was no longer any need to go borrow more "candy" just to perform the operations we already knew were in the best interest of the company.

That meant acquisitions!

CHAPTER 31
Go Shopping

In 2009, flush with this monetary infusion, we went out on the prowl for companies we could buy.

The first acquisition we made—in addition to the original Ligouri and Associate takeover, of course—was a small company in Northern California. The entire process couldn't have gone more smoothly. We were just getting our feet wet, just getting used to the procedures and protocols, but the whole transaction went off without a hitch. More importantly, the resulting synergies and other benefits were amazing—and exactly what the company needed.

My appetite was whetted.

Now we started looking at companies even more aggressively. And this meant that we were widening our geographic scope as well, not just concentrating on California, but also considering companies in Arizona and Colorado, as well.

What I quickly learned about acquisitions was that even the smoothest of them are still difficult and demanding transactions that necessarily require a lot of time from start to finish. So, I was running all over this extended region that we'd set out for ourselves, meeting with people, and

Someone had to be in the driver's seat there, too, to make sure that the engine of this machine was running smoothly.

trying to put deals together. At the same time, however, I still had the same day-to-day responsibilities of running a company with revenues that were now over $200 million. Someone had to be in the driver's seat there, too, to make sure that the engine of this machine was running smoothly. That required an enormous amount of time and effort, too.

Between the time that I needed to spend running the company and the time I was spending developing acquisitions—well, there just wasn't enough time. After a period of trying to keep this impossible schedule, I came to the conclusion that we needed to bring in a full-time employee to handle acquisitions.

The big question was—who?

About this time, I received a call from a woman I had first met as a realtor. She had sold my house for me several years earlier and she was calling to see if she could set up a meeting with me. She explained that despite her degree in finance and her MBA, the bursting of the real estate bubble had necessitated her transferring her skills to the financial staffing industry and she wanted to know if she could speak to me about future prospects. I was curious about a realtor having such a deep financial background and we arranged to meet for lunch.

Over the course of our discussion, she explained that she had been a CFO for a family business and she'd overseen a number of acquisitions on their behalf. Unfortunately, her father's deteriorating health had necessitated the sale of the family business.

I smiled and nodded ... because I knew—I've said it before and I believe it as strongly as any of the other truths I've proven to myself during my business career: you might be able to screen a large crop of candidates according to their resumes, but you have to hire the one you want based on your gut feeling. Sitting there at lunch, I just knew instinctively that she was the right person to lead our acquisition team. I had that feeling in my gut that she was the only one who could do it the way that I knew it needed to be done.

I told her to forget about financial staffing. She looked surprised. I explained her the we had just gotten a whole lot of money and we needed to go on an aggressive course of multiple acquisitions. I told her that I wanted her to lead the charge and I offered her the job right there on the spot.

She told me that she needed time to think about it—which was really the only prudent and reasonable response she could offer—but it wasn't that much later that she called me to discuss the offer in detail.

Her first question was simply to inquire if I was serious in my offer. I told her I was dead serious—(which I almost always am). She confessed that she'd originally thought I must be full of it, but that if I was committed to doing something real, she was willing to give the situation a try.

I thought the whole course of events was working out perfectly. Brian, however, had his reservations about my decision. He wanted someone with more traditional acquisition experience. I explained to him that she did have some acquisition experience, but more than that she had all of the intangible qualities we needed for someone to take on this position.

Brian hedged on her hiring, so I set up a meeting for them. The minute Brian met her the debate ended. She came aboard and we got to work on growing the company.

The first year of our aggressive strategy was 2010, and we purchased four separate companies, spending a total of $22 million dollars. Two companies in Arizona, one in Texas, and one in our backyard in Southern California.

That's $22 million dollars at 19 percent interest. Do the math. That's a lot of cash being spent on interest payments.

We were under tremendous pressure to make all of those deals work out. Not only did we need them to keep our growth rate ahead of the interest rate, but I was also aware that from a motivational standpoint we needed to get some significant wins under our belt. At the same time, our sales team was killing themselves and largely through their hard work we were sustaining about 30 percent organic growth.

So, between our acquisitions that year and our organic growth, we added about $60 million in annual revenues. It was just unheard-of growth in the industry.

The entire team had been running a million miles an hour to get it all done. The year 2010 had been a fantastic year, a fabulous year. And when it came to an end, all I could think was that we had to do even better in 2011.

CHAPTER 32
Hire the Best

The thing about the security business is that while we operate within a multi-billion-dollar industry, behind the scenes it's really something of a small town in which everyone knows everyone.

Over the course of my time in the industry, I had developed a friendly relationship with a guy who owned a business in North Carolina, which obviously was *waaaaaay* out of the geographic region we had been focusing on. Nevertheless, I was aware that it was a great company with about $80 million in annual revenues and offices in North Carolina, Georgia, and Florida. We were having dinner one night and—just like I had during my dinner with Lou Ligouri—I asked him what his future plans were, more motivated by generating friendly conversation than exploring acquisition options. He told me that he had just brought his daughter into the business, but there was something about our talk that led me to believe that maybe his fire for the business had died down just a little.

Intrigued by the possibilities, I invited his daughter and him out to California and wined and dined them. We took in a Lakers game. Everything went perfectly.

The next day, the three of us got together in our offices and started talking for real. Before I knew what had happened, I was shaking their hands to seal the deal we had just negotiated.

It was one of those moments when things just go more quickly than you'd ever thought they would. When I had started the courtship, I had assumed that there would be some time involved, a period that would allow everyone to get aligned with the acquisition. I'd never suspected it could happen so quickly.

Now, however, I had to go into Brian's office with the news and by this time I think he was just afraid to see me stick my head through his door. It was like he just knew something else was coming at him unexpectedly.

There's no easy way to tell your partner that you just bought a business all the way across the country, so I didn't sugar-coat it. I just told him. For a minute, I think maybe Brian thought about killing me. A moment later he had settled on trusting me. Again.

We borrowed $30 million dollars to get the deal done—again, at 19 percent interest—and suddenly we owned companies on both coasts.

Acquiring the company had been a real coup, but making the deal work— (i.e., maximizing synergies, rebranding, realizing revenue)—all of that took an enormous amount of the company's energies and required me to fly back and forth between the coasts constantly.

The real world is very different from what they teach you in school.

Now, I think any case study for business school would conclude that the proper step at this particular junction would be for the company to slow down and focus on what they'd already acquired, just sort of swallow what they'd bit off. That would, of course, have been the prudent course. That would have been the A+ answer in any business school exam.

But the real world is very different from what they teach you in school. We did the exact opposite.

I went out and doubled-down on our commitment to grow the company through acquisitions. By this time, however, I was more

172

or less living on an airplane and our acquisition department was working full tilt, all of the time. I knew that we needed help.

One of our biggest clients—in fact, if you'll remember the client that started it all for me—was the Irvine Company. Over the course of doing business with them, I had developed a particularly strong friendship with their VP of operations, Steve Claton.

Steve, I knew, was my kind of guy. I also knew I wanted him to be a part of the Universal team.

Like the NFL's prohibitions on talking to a member of another team's coaching staff until after the season is over, I cleared all of the hurdles with the Irvine Company to make sure they were okay with my intentions and then I raised the idea of coming to work for us with Steve. Steve told me that he appreciated my interest, by he was already a VP of operations with a multi-billion-dollar company and there was a lot to consider in coming over to join Universal Protection, a company at the time that had revenues in the neighborhood of $300 million.

Even though there was a distinct difference in the size of the companies at that time, I knew Steve was enough like me that he was intrigued about the prospects of what could be done to build up Universal Protection to meet my vision and expectations; the adventure of building a company up all by ourselves.

Still, despite his interest in the exciting possibilities, Steve had a family and a child on the way and he was very understandably focused on those responsibilities. And those responsibilities, I knew, were the key. I invited Steve and his wife to dinner. I explained that we'd be paying him more. He was flattered, but ...

I outlined my plan for the future of the company and for those individuals who were part of that building process. He was intrigued, but ...

I knew I had to do something. And I knew exactly what that was. On the way home from dinner, I took a little "detour" through one of the nicest neighborhoods in … well, in my opinion, in all of the United States. We drove up and down street after street, each house that we passed was nicer than the next.

And then I pulled up to one house that was particularly stunning. It was all lit up on that beautiful night … and there was a FOR SALE sign in the front yard. I turned to Steve and his wife in the backseat. "If you come to work for us, this house could be yours."

I saw the same doubt and hesitation in Steve's eyes, but his wife's eyes were absolutely set and certain. Steve came to work for us shortly thereafter.

CHAPTER 33
Go, Go, Go!

Having Steve join the team was a huge step forward for Universal Protection. I gave him everything between California and Texas to handle and he did a great job of wrapping his arms around it all and taking it off of my plate.

Of course, that didn't necessarily make my work day any shorter, it merely gave me more time to keep running around the country looking for companies to acquire trying to figure out how Universal was going to build a national footprint.

Everything was going great, but Brian was growing increasingly concerned by the hectic pace we were all running at. He told me, "Steve, we just bought all of these companies. We've expanded into the southeast. We just have to slow down."

I understood what he was saying but, respectfully, I also knew that he was wrong. "This isn't the time to slow down," I told him. "We've got to keep our foot on the accelerator and pin it to the floor. We're going to take over the security industry and you just have to trust me."

He gave me that look, a look I had come to know very well in our time together. The look that said, "Steve, I'm getting too old for this go, go, go and taking risk after risk, but you've never steered me wrong yet … so I trust you on this."

A few weeks later, I think I might have given him reason to reconsider that position. We'd already firmly established ourselves in California and the Southwest, but with the spread to the Southeast, it seemed only logical to me that we had to fill in the hole in the middle. And so, we set out to acquire a company in the Midwest.

We found the perfect one and closed as quickly as we could. This new addition to Universal Protection, particularly an acquisition in a geographic market that we had never explored before, really tested Brian's risk tolerance to the max. He got over the shock, of course, but I think somewhere along the line he expressed the opinion that our Midwest addition should have been the last acquisition for the year ... but you know what they say about *should've*s.

Like a Christmas present I didn't even know I wanted that year, this great company in New York City came up for sale in December. New York City!

I knew that adding this company would have been a perfect fit for our growing company, a presence in Manhattan, so I pursued the deal as hard as I could. I flew the company CEO out to California and we sat down to talk. Everything went perfectly and it seemed to me like the deal was a lock. That is, until Brian learned what I was up to.

We had one of "those" meetings in his office and he told me, "Look, I've trusted you every step of the way. And although I still trust you, I've got to put my foot down here. We just opened up the Southeast. And now the Midwest. It's just too much. So, about this New York City merger, I just gotta say—no."

"Excuse me?"

"No." He stared back at me. He was adamant. "No" meant "no."

That is, except to me in matters of business. In that case, "no" just meant, "You're going to have to find another way to get what you want."

It turned out that the way to convince Brian was simply to invite him to New York City. We went out, sat down with the CEO and his people, toured the company, and Brian's take-away was the same as mine. We *had* to have that company.

There was just one problem. "Steve, how is this even possible?" Brian asked. "We just closed the deal in North Carolina. Then the Midwest. And now you want to move into the Northeast, too? We're borrowing all of this money at 19 percent interest. I just don't see how we can possibly get this done."

I, of course, had a vision. I explained everything for him. I set out how we were going to make the transition. I worked out everything and made sure each and every piece was lined up perfectly. At the same time, I was negotiating with the owner until we had absolutely all of the fine points locked down tight on that end, too.

After all of this, we rightfully considered ourselves serious veterans of the acquisition game and I was absolutely certain that there were no obstacles to moving forward. So, I was more than a little surprised when we went to our financial partners at Caltius and they came back with a big fat, "No."

I was taken aback. "What do you mean, 'No?'"

Their reply was simple and to the point. "Look, you've borrowed $100 million dollars. We're only a $500 million fund. Our guidelines restrict us from lending more than 20 percent of the fund to any one company. In fact, we weren't supposed to loan you more than 10 percent of the fund, but we just fell in love with your company. If it was up to us, we'd be in on this deal, too. We'd invest everything with you. We just can't. You're by far the biggest investment we've ever made."

This idea of a "maximum" to our financing was a new one to me. "What do you mean? I've got an acquisition in New York City that we are ready to close on. Thanks for telling me now."

I think I have already made clear what "No" means to me when we're talking business.

Now, I was aware that anyone else in my position would have taken the fund's refusal to extend us the necessary financing as a sign that we needed to slow down. I, however, saw it as a sign that I needed to find an alternate source of financing.

Anyone else in my position would have taken the fund's refusal to extend us the necessary financing as a sign that we needed to slow down. I, however, saw it as a sign that I needed to find an alternate source of financing.

Our people at Caltius came back to us and reiterated that they were confident about the loan, but that their hands were tied. To help us move ahead with the acquisition, they offered to introduce us to one of their own investors, Partners Group, which from time to time got involved in side investments. I decided take them up on their offer and we scheduled a meeting for me to sit down with members of Partners Group.

They were obviously familiar with what the company had done, but I walked them through the entire Universal Protection story, from starting out as a twleve-million-dollar, family-run company all the way through the present day when we were a 600-million-dollar company with offices across the country. I explained to them what we had planned for the future and how we were going to make Universal Protection into a billion-dollar company.

At the end of the meeting, I had all of the money I needed to close on the New York City acquisition. Partners Group, an investor in our original mezzanine fund, had agreed to loan us $30 million —at 19 percent interest.

The acquisition of a company in New York City made Universal Protection Service a legitimate national company. If we weren't in every city quite yet, we were certainly in every region. The company was now at about $700 million in annual revenues. By any metric, it was a remarkable development, particularly for a twleve-million-dollar, family-run company that I had become a part of just fifteen years earlier.

I suppose anyone else would've seen all of this as an achievement to celebrate. Brian certainly did. He sat me down. "Look, we've made sixteen acquisitions in just a couple of years. It's been a helluva run and we've accomplished so much more than I ever thought we could when we first started down this road together. But now this company has grown so large that I just think that maybe it's time that that we take advantage of everything that we've built, cash in, and sell out."

I wasn't sure how to tell Brian that over the course of my career I had learned that there were basically (down deep at their core) two kinds of people in business: Those who want to sell. And those who want to buy. By my very nature, I just wasn't someone who wanted to sell. "Sell, Brian? This isn't the end of anything. I'm only just getting started."

CHAPTER 34
Make Good on The Dream

At the beginning of 2013, I got a phone call from Brett White, someone whom I had met when he was the CEO of CBRE, the world's largest commercial real estate services company, with offices in one hundred countries and assets in excess of $10 billion. Under Brett's leadership, CBRE had been a very important client for Universal.

Brett let me know that he'd just retired from his position at CBRE. He told me that before he'd left that position, he had talked to the property managers at all of his North American properties about security and they all told him that without a doubt the best in the business was Universal Protection Service.

Brett asked if we could have a meeting. I answered, "Of course," and we sat down to talk. He explained that among his many achievements at CBRE, he had been instrumental in taking the company public. Now that he had retired, however, he was looking for another opportunity to be a part of building something great. He was as to-the-point as I would've expected someone who had achieved Brett's level of success would be. "Look, I'd like to buy into your business."

Brian and I weren't necessarily looking for another partner, but over the course of our meeting, Brett convinced me to at least take a trip to New York with him. (Yup, the ol' "Trip to New York" trick.)

Brett was beyond gracious about the entire situation. He told Brian and me that if we didn't want to be his partner, he could understand that position, but he loved what we had done with our company so much that he wanted the opportunity to introduce us to some of the biggest private equity groups in the world, just to show us how we could do it on our own.

Brett made all of the introductions, and Brian and I took five meetings with five different private equity groups. At the end of the day, all five wanted to invest in Universal Protection.

Of the five groups, the one that was obviously the most interested was Warburg Pincus, an international private equity firm that had an established track record of having raised fifteen private equity funds which have invested $58 billion in more than 760 companies in more than forty countries.

Shortly after we got home from New York, the folks from Warburg Pincus called me up and said that they were coming out to California to play golf and that they wanted me to join them. I explained that I didn't have time for golf but asked if we could meet over dinner instead. I showed up at the Pelican Hill Resort and we had dinner in one of the lavish villas on property. As we ate dinner and discussed Universal, one of the partners, Chandler Reedy, sat at a side table capturing our negotiations on his laptop and then right there on the spot, with his portable printer, he presented us with a letter of intent to buy Universal.

Now I am an incredibly aggressive guy, but even I was impressed with the print-while-you-wait document offer. It was a bold move and a meeting I'll never forgot. I told everyone that Brian and I needed some time to think over the proposed deal and they graciously understood.

The next afternoon, I got another call from Brett. It was obvious to me that he still wanted an opportunity to invest in the business, but there was also a true mentoring spirit within him as he talked me through the options that we had in front of us. He told me, "Steve, you're going to have your dream. You're going to build Universal Protection into a billion-dollar company. You're going to take this company public. It'll be everything you wanted. It's just a matter of time. You just need to move wisely now."

Over the course of our conversation, we stumbled over the fact that Brett's wife and I had gone to high school in Irvine together. Brett said that they were in Los Angeles and they wanted to know if they could take my wife and me to brunch the next morning.

We had a long conversation over brunch and it became increasingly clear to me that he could see—really *see*—my vision for the company.

Just a word here: When you have a vision for something like I had for Universal Protection growing into the industry-dominating giant that I wanted it to be, you have to be true to that vision because most people won't be able to see it the same way that you do. Even if they trust in you personally and follow you into the fray, you're still left alone with your vision.

> When you have a vision for something like I had for Universal Protection growing into the industry-dominating giant that I wanted it to be, you have to be true to that vision because most people won't be able to see it the same way that you do.

And so, I can't begin to express what an enormous feeling of relief it was to sit down with Brett and have someone else share that vision with me, to have someone else who could see the exact same thing that I had been seeing by myself for all of those years.

The experience was like when I was playing football and I would get a chance to come in off of the field for just a minute to maybe catch my breath and have a quick drink of Gatorade. Thirty seconds to refresh, revitalize, and get ready to go back out there and continue to grind.

I left the brunch with Brett and his wife more convinced than ever that not only was my vision legitimate, but also that I was on the right path to turn it into something real. When I returned to the office, however, it became equally clear that Brian was finding it increasingly difficult to follow me (and my vision.)

To be completely fair, I certainly can't say that I didn't understand his point of view—I just couldn't go along with it. Brian and I had been together from the beginning and whether he had believed in my vision or not, he had always believed in me. Because of that singular faith, he had put all of his chips on me every single time I came to the line. I cannot imagine ever having a better partner and certainly none of the success that Universal Protection had achieved would have been possible without his invaluable contributions to the company.

Brian, however, was satisfied with what we had done.

And all of that phenomenal success—particularly at a time when much of the global economy had been undergoing a crisis more significant than any seen since the days of the Great Depression—was nothing short of a business miracle. So, I don't think there's anyone who could blame him for wanting to sit back and take full advantage of the rewards that type of success brings. Or, at least, I could never blame him. I'd always understood completely.

The fact of the matter, however, is that I didn't want to sit back. Or, more to the point, I couldn't sit back. Not ever. I had a vision and I needed to do whatever it took to realize it fully.

I went back to Partners Group, who had come through for us with the New York City acquisition and I told them, "Listen, we're tapped out with Caltius, but we've got more acquisitions that we need to do to get our company where it needs to be. I'm thinking about doing a deal with a private equity firm; what can you guys do for us."

They considered my proposal and then came back with an offer of their own. "We're also a private equity group. We do debt and private equity. In fact, we're one of the largest private equity funds in the world with more than $50 billion under management. We're headquartered in Switzerland, but we'd love to have one of our representatives come out and sit down with you to talk things over."

A week later I met with this guy. Sharp guy. Mature. Supersmart. He said, "My name is Dave Layton. I'm with Partner's Group, on the private equity side. I understand that you've already talked with some potential private equity partners, what's your hesitation?"

Explaining the true nature of our hesitation was difficult, but I set out for him that there was a shared concern about working so hard to build our business and then turning it over to an interest that we didn't have a personal relationship with.

Dave understood. "Look, if you'd rather, we could do a minority interest in Universal Protection, but one way or another we'd really like the opportunity to invest with you."

I talked the prospect over with Brian and he told me, "Steve, I've been with you, I've been at your side for all of this. It's been a crazy ride and I am so glad that I got a chance to take it with you. We've achieved more than I ever thought possible, but I really think it's time to take some chips off of the table."

It was hard to hear (again), but this time I realized that I couldn't keep telling him that he was wrong when what he was telling me wasn't what he wanted, but what he *needed* out of the situation. I took a deep breath and then told Dave to see what he could work out.

Dave came back to me with a proposal that would have sold Partners Group a majority stake in Universal Protection, with me staying on and remaining the largest individual shareholder. It was a good deal, I knew. But I also knew that Brian and I were only going to get one shot at selling what we had worked so hard to build and I wanted to hit the bullseye. Dead center.

I told Dave that we were flattered by the deal, but that we didn't think it reflected everything that Universal Protection had achieved. If anything, Dave was well prepared for that response and he showed us all of the comps for other businesses in the industry that he had assembled.

"I know," I admitted, "but the thing is that Universal Protection isn't like any other business out there. It's something special and that intangible quality is what I don't see reflected in the offer." As it happened, we were holding these negotiations right around the time of the annual security industry convention (the one that I missed for the birth of my youngest son when it was in Atlanta).

I asked Dave to fly out to Las Vegas with Brian, our VP of Acquisitions, and me, just to observe what it was that made Universal Protection so special—and so much more valuable than the comps and figures could ever capture.

While we were in Vegas, we took four meetings with four different companies and, by the end of our time there, three of the four companies had signed Letters of Intent for us to acquire them.

Dave was shocked at the results we were able to achieve in just a couple of days. "Okay, I'm in. Let me figure out how I'm going to convince my partners in Switzerland, but don't worry I'll convince them. I'll pay you guys what you're asking because I've never seen anything like it. It's a little bit of a risk, but I'm all in."

Dave flew back to Switzerland and a couple of days later I got a call. "I need a favor. I need you guys to fly out here to Switzerland to meet my partners. They think I'm paying too much for the company, but I've told them that once they meet you they will understand why."

So, Brian, our CFO, VP of acquisitions, and I, the four of us, climbed on a plane and flew over to Switzerland. We had a meeting and I told them the Universal Protection story. Next thing I knew, the four of us were in Zurich celebrating the record-breaking deal we had just made. Since we were in Switzerland, we all got watches to mark the occasion.

So 2013 was coming to an end and suddenly Brian and I had our asking price for the company on our own terms. Brian was still involved, but basically, he got the cash out he had wanted for so long. I got to remain as CEO, not only calling the plays for the company, but also remaining as the largest single shareholder.

I was finally able to pay off all of the high-interest mezzanine loans that the company had taken.

And, perhaps most important of all, and I got a $50 billion-dollar best friend in Switzerland with some very, very deep pockets.

The time had come. Now, I knew I was finally in position to make good on the dream.

CHAPTER 35
Be a Legend

In 2013, Universal Protection Service was growing at an unheard of rate of something in the neighborhood of 40–50 percent. My only thought was, "Now that we have the financial capacity and flexibility to go out and really grow, how do we accelerate our growth?"

The short answer to that question was that we really had to put the foot down on the accelerator to hype up the growth on a company that was already growing at an unprecedented rate. By this time, we were a national company and we had offices in four major regions. I was acutely aware, however, that there were a number of significant holes in our jigsaw puzzle map of the United States. I was determined to fix that.

As a result, our entire company became dedicated to filling in those gaps by spreading the company across the entire United States. Our sales team, which had done an amazing job in whatever region they had been set loose on, transitioned into becoming a national sales force, with a team that blanketed the entire US. Their results proved that there were no geographic borders to what they could accomplish.

At the same time, I took to the air again, flying back and forth across the country both looking to develop clients and searching for businesses that we could acquire. Within two years, by the end of 2015, all of our combined hard work had resulted in taking the company from about $750 million in annual revenues to just over

$1.5 billion. We had just about doubled the company's revenue in under twenty-four months.

And that put me in a position to go after the biggest target of all. Captain Ahab had Moby Dick; I had Allied-Barton.

At the time, Allied-Barton were vying with us to be the biggest player in the game and I knew that if I could acquire them, then not only would Universal stand alone at the very top of the mountain, but also all of the smaller companies would fall into place for us.

I went after Allied-Barton with everything that I had. I got them to the table twice, too. Both of those times, we made it through all of the negotiations but on the very day that the papers were set to be signed, the deal fell apart and Allied-Barton's CEO walked away from the deal.

Twice!

I think more than any substantive issues, the stumbling blocks to closing those deals just came down to their CEO not wanting to announce that they had been acquired by Universal. So, I felt there was an element of something more than "just business" involved in our interactions and the second time this happened to me, I felt like an entire offensive line had just spent an hour running up and down my back. Crushed. Really crushed.

I felt like an entire offensive line had just spent an hour running up and down my back. Crushed.

I was trying to figure out what Universal's next step could be and thought I might benefit from some advice, so I called up one of the smartest guys I knew and one of the few that I can honestly say may work just a little (very little) bit harder than I do.

I'd met Dave Layton working out the Partners Group deal, but since that time we had developed a genuine friendship that I value greatly to this day.

"I need some strategic help here," I told him. "Allied-Barton just walked out on us for the second time. I just can't go back there and take the same defeat for a third time. I need a plan for moving forward that doesn't involve them."

To help me out, Dave flew to Los Angeles and we got together in a business club there. It was just the two of us and a white board and together we listed out every major acquisition that Universal Protection could possibly make at that time. Every single one of them.

The next day I took my list and got to work. The first name on my list was Guardsmark. It was a good-sized business that had annual revenues around $500 million, but the company was more than just the numbers, because it was just an absolute legend in the security industry. Guardsmark was headquartered in Manhattan and headed by a guy named Ira Lipman, who was personally every bit the legend that his company was. Guardsmark was such a special company that over time absolutely everyone in the industry had tried to buy it at one time or another. Most contenders couldn't even get a meeting with Mr. Lipman.

I had a friend who was an investment banker who enjoyed a relationship with Mr. Lipman and I asked him to set up a meeting. He agreed. A couple days later I got word that Mr. Lipman had agreed to meet me for dinner.

On the date in question I had one of those travel days when absolutely everything that can go wrong did go wrong. The flight was late getting out of LAX and later still getting into JFK. It took forever for the car to get into the city. And all this time I was just running and running to get to this very important meeting. By the time I finally made it to the restaurant, I was late (a personal pet peeve of Mr. Lipman), and I looked like I'd made the trip in the trunk of the town car.

One of the many special things about Mr. Lipman was that no matter the day or the hour, he always wore a full suit and tie. Folded pocket square. Everything. Immaculate. As I rushed into the restaurant, I half feared the man was simply going to have me thrown out.

I think because of that, because I was as good as certain that circumstances beyond my control had soured my first impression, I did away with whatever introduction I had practiced during the long trip out and simply sat down as myself, tired and hungry and eager just for the opportunity to spend a meal talking with one of the last true legends of the industry. There was no deference; I just told him the Universal Protection story and expressed my desire to add his company to our ever-growing company.

He didn't throw me out that night. In fact, it was the beginning of a personal friendship and a professional courtship.

For the next three months, I would fly out to NYC every Tuesday and stay at the hotel right next to his apartment building. We would have dinner on Tuesday night and then lunch on Wednesday. Every week. For three months. At the end of that time, however, Mr. Lipman had agreed to sell Guardsmark to me.

This wasn't just another acquisition for me. Mr. Lipman had started Guardsmark more than fifty years earlier and built it up from the ground in the toughest city in the world. The company was a true labor of love. It meant the world to him.

So, while we eventually worked out all of the numbers and figures, settled on agreeable terms and conditions, I'd like to believe that there was something much more to the arrangement that we reached than just another acquisition. I'd like to believe that Mr.

Lipman knew that he could trust me with his company, not only to continue the success it had always enjoyed, but to carry on the same spirit that had made it a legendary business in the first place. I certainly felt (and continue to feel) that responsibility.

And so, to me at least, it was more of a changing of the guards than an acquisition.

CHAPTER 36
You Can Never Have
Too Many Partners

The Guardsmark acquisition was a sentimental achievement for me, but to the rest of the industry—and those who kept their eyes on it—the deal was absolutely the biggest acquisition of the era.

No one could believe that I had managed to pull it off. And the fact I had done "the impossible" (again) set everyone to talking.

One of those talking the loudest was Chandler Reedy from Warburg Pincus, the private equity firm that had wined and dined us and blew me away with the type-the-offer-at-the-dinner-table move that I never forgot. They asked if we could talk again about Warburg buying Universal.

> No one could believe that I had managed to pull it off. And the fact I had done "the impossible" (again) set everyone to talking.

They were shocked that we had been able to double Universal Protection in just the two years since we had last talked and they were very interested in a relationship that would allow them to partner with us.

And they knew just exactly what to say to get my full attention. "We want to be a part of your continued success. We know the most obvious business to acquire now is Allied-Barton. So we would like to partner with you to go and buy Allied-Barton together."

You had me at Allied-Barton.

I explained that I had already been down that road before. Twice. And that both times they had pulled some simple, minor thread and unraveled the entire deal in the twelfth hour. Twice. I explained, instead, that Dave Layton and I had come up with a list of acquisition targets and I explained my determination to methodically cross off each entry on my list. Including Guardsmark.

They were so impressed that they responded with an offer to buy the company. "We want to buy the company. We'll pay a premium and we can close quickly. What do you say?"

I knew the decision wasn't entirely mine and so I sat them down with representatives from Partners Group and all three of us discussed the possibilities for all of us moving forward. Together.

Eventually, we all reached a deal in which Warburg Pincus would buy Universal Protection, while Partners Group would remain a partner with their initial investment but would take their profits off of the table. (It was an enormous profit for them.) The deal we reached was a win-win-win.

On August 1, 2015, we announced that Universal Protection had been bought by Warburg Pincus, one of the largest private equity funds in the world *and* that we had closed on the Guardsmark acquisition. It was a big news day.

But the very next day, I was back to my list.

The next name on my list was ABM Security, a subsidiary of ABM Industries, a $5.1 billion-dollar company. I went straight to work and made the deal as quickly as I could. When all of the pieces were in place, I went to my new private equity partners at Warburg

Pincus. They seemed surprised to hear back from me so quickly and shocked that I was coming to them with another acquisition.

They said, "It's only been ninety days since you bought Guardsmark, do you really think you can handle another merger?"

"Absolutely." And with that we checked ABM Security off of my list.

Over the course of 2015 we acquired more than a billion dollars worth of business. I figured that was a good start.

It was good to have a private equity partner that was every bit as aggressive as I was and one who backed my vision of making Universal Protection the number one player in the market. The lead on our deal was none other than Mr. Printer-at-the-dinner-table, Chandler Reedy. In a mere six months together, we acquired the number six and number seven largest companies in our industry.

Again, not a bad start, but it was just a start!

CHAPTER 37
Manage Your Expectations

The last days of 2015 brought some other exciting news, as well. Allied-Barton had just been sold to Wendel, a French private equity group.

I got a call from Chandler Reedy at Warburg Pincus, "What do you think? Should we go out and try to buy Allied-Barton?" They didn't have to ask me twice.

We approached Wendel with an offer to buy Allied-Barton outright, but having just acquired them, they weren't interested in letting the company go. What they did have an interest in was the possibility of putting the two companies together. A merger.

The possibilities seemed intriguing and, certainly, all of Universal's private equity partners wanted to get the deal done. The problem was that as we opened up a dialogue on the subject, the same issues that had prevented us from acquiring Allied-Barton before seemed to raise their ugly heads for a third time. As Yogi Berra once observed, "It was *deja vu* all over again."

Personally, I was ready to walk away and return to my list of acquisition targets, but our private equity people asked me to try one last time. I reached out to Allied-Barton's CEO and asked for a meeting. He let it be known that he was on a very limited time frame and suggested that we meet "halfway" … in Memphis, of all places.

I was in Santa Ana, California. He was in Conshohocken, Pennsylvania. I was pretty sure that "halfway" wasn't Memphis, but with what was at stake I also wasn't going to be bothered arguing about mileage and flight time.

Fine, Memphis.

He set a morning meeting, so I left California at the break of dawn to make it to Memphis by 7:00 a.m. We talked for a while but it seemed to me that we were never going to get anywhere. Still, I stayed in the negotiations and eventually we came to an agreement.

Nothing about that ultimate deal inclined me to take my foot up off of the accelerator.

Allied-Barton's CEO shook my hand, told me it was his birthday and that he was going to Florida to play golf. Then he was gone.

And that was all there was to it. After all that time, the most anticipated acquisition of my career thus far turned out to be the most anticlimactic of them all.

I stood there in Memphis and thought about just how far I had actually come to get to that point. And just like that we had created Allied-Universal, a $4.5 billion company and the single largest player in the security guarding industry in all of North America.

The deal closed on August 1, 2016—it was exactly a year to the day that we had announced our deal with Warburg-Pincus and our acquisition of Guardsmark.

To many, that would have seemed to be the crowning jewel, but nothing about that ultimate deal inclined me to take my foot up off of the accelerator.

CHAPTER 38
Make the Tough Decisions

After the rapid success of acquisitions we had completed, my team was fatigued. They had all bought into my plan completely, supported my vision, and they had given their all to make all of that success possible. And then the merger with Allied-Barton was announced.

The news shook the industry, but it obviously had very strong reverberations within my own organization as well. As Universal's CEO, I knew I had a responsibility to sit down with everyone within my organization and explain to them why the merger was good for the company as a whole and what it meant to them personally.

And that was the difficult conversation for all of us to have, because for the first time in my career there was a real possibility that certain people within Universal would potentially be losing their jobs. This time their celebrations were tempered with very real concerns for themselves and their workmates. That's the painful difference between a merger and an acquisition.

With the acquisition process, we almost always kept the Universal Protection people in place and displaced the redundant employees from the acquired company. To the victors go the spoils.

This time was different.

At the time, we had 70,000 employees at Universal Protection. Allied-Barton brought in 60,000 employees of their own. To bring them together into a single workforce would certainly be an enormous task—but a painful one, as well.

To provide an example of the work that we were facing—and the real world consequences of which we were painfully aware—when we began the process, there were 300 offices between us. By the time we were done, we had worked that down to just 180.

This time I had to explain to everyone on the respective executive teams, Universal and Allied-Barton alike, that I was going to be sitting down and interviewing everyone. In essence, it was like tryouts from my football years and I likened it to the times when the 49ers brought Steve Young in while Joe Montana was still with the team, or when the Packers signed Aaron Rogers to "back up" Brett Favre.

And what made the process of choosing a team from all of the potential candidates even more difficult was that everyone came from two very different cultures: Allied-Barton had been an old and established company that had been owned for a long time by one private equity company or another for years and relied solely on slow, steady growth. Universal was a very different beast, altogether.

They were mature, with the same procedures and protocols in place for decades. We were the new upstarts, who could run-and-gun better than anyone on the block. It was two very different worlds and I had the task of bringing them together into one.

I understood the importance of making this decision on what could be considered neutral ground, without giving the candidates from either company an unfair advantage. I chose Dallas—(much closer to "the middle" than Memphis had been)—and brought in all of the executive leaders for both teams.

It was an uneasy gathering and so I felt it necessary to start things out with an introductory talk about what we were going to be doing in our selection process and why it was necessary for all of them to go through with it. I told them all what we were trying to build with the merged companies, what the new company would look like, and where we intended to take it into the future.

Most of all, I stressed that while Allied-Universal was now the biggest security company in North America, bigger didn't necessarily mean better. I made another football analogy and explained that the big, strong, and fast player generally finds himself drafted in the NFL, but the big, slow, and uncoordinated player finds himself getting sent home after college. I understood what everyone in the room was feeling, but I stressed that we had to all come together to create a new company—a blend of the best of both—that would continue to provide the very best security services to our customers in every market.

Then I started the interviews.

For two straight days, I participated in twelve hours of interview after interview after interview. I talked to everyone to determine who was the best fit at their position in the new company. It was a daunting task, but it was just the start of the long, hard road that lay ahead of us. In the end, I made the best decisions that I could make, although each and every selection was a difficult choice to make.

What mattered most to me in the process was that we conducted ourselves with the utmost class and that we treated all of these valued executives fairly.

We let them all know as quickly as possible what our decision was so that the inevitable worry in such a situation wasn't continued unnecessarily. For those who did not make the cut, we made sure that there were (more than) generous severance packages in place so that none of them would have any concern about providing for their families in the near future. We helped with placing them in other positions wherever we could. And in these most trying circumstances, we treated each and every one of those candidates like the superstars that they were. And I will say that handling the matter in this way was not only the right thing to do in the situation, but it returned some very practical and real-world rewards.

What mattered most to me in the process was that we conducted ourselves with the utmost class and that we treated all of these valued executives fairly.

I firmly believe that if you treat someone decently, then you will receive the benefits of those actions. There were serious business considerations in play that forced our hands into making tough decisions out of sheer necessity. There was simply nothing else that we could do. But the way that we handled it—professionally and with class—was returned to us by these individuals every step of the way.

As a result, every one of these individuals stayed at their position until the transitory phase of the merger had been completed and did a fantastic job in facilitating those changes. Because both those who were chosen to continue with the Allied-Universal team and those who were not made a commitment to moving forward, the merger was an enormous success.

CHAPTER 39
Be the Leader

When I conducted those interviews in Dallas, I was looking for people who could not only do their jobs but fit into my team. I was looking for leaders.

Leadership. A lot has been written on the topic, both in the more academic journals as well as in more mainstream magazines and books. Everybody these days seems to have a philosophy on the qualities that make for a good leader.

While I've read much of what has been written and subscribe to a lot of it, I have to confess that much of my own personal philosophy on leadership, like so many of the other qualities that make me the businessman that I am, are derived from lessons that I learned out on the football field. They may be simple, but they have served me well.

More importantly, these lessons have shaped me into a man that people want to work for and people want to invest in. In my estimation, there is no better "real world" test of someone's leadership abilities than that.

The first component that every leader must possess is a vision of the future. That is, you have to know where you're going to take your business and how you're going to get it there.

I can promise you that every team's fortunes are set for failure or success long before one foot is set out on the playing field on Opening Day. Championships are not the result of one player's exceptional performance, they are earned by an entire team executing the roles they have been assigned in bringing their coach's game plan to fruition.

Business is no different. There are a thousand factors that will impact your company's performance in the marketplace, but the degree of success that you ultimately achieve is determined almost exclusively by your vision for the future and your plan of action for transforming those plans into something real.

The first component that every leader must possess is a vision of the future.

Simply having such a plan is not enough, however. If you can't effectively convey that plan to your team in such a way that they buy in, then your plan is just a plan. There are two steps to this. The first is to communicate effectively. If your people don't understand what you want them to do, what you expect of them, then they cannot be expected to accomplish those tasks. There has to be a clear understanding between you and your people so that when it comes time for game day and they step out on the field, their minds aren't cluttered with *"What should I be doing?"* but are focused clearly on doing everything that needs to be done in order to execute on their assignments. That's step one. Step two is much, much more difficult. Step two requires you to set out your game plan in such a way that everyone in your organization buys into it and commits to it, 110 percent.

If you have ever seen a team that was stacked with all-star talent but not only failed to realize their championship potential but imploded into a mess of scandal and finger-pointing, I can promise you that the core of the problem was that the team did not collectively buy into the coach's game plan for the season.

So, contrary to what might have been the methods of yesterday when Coach Vince Lombardi could chew out his team and transform them to champions or a CEO could simply bark orders, today's leaders need to exercise a great deal more emotional intelligence and business savvy. You can't simply demand that people follow you and expect that anyone of the personal character and caliber you want on your team will simply get in line behind you. To the contrary, particularly in today's market, getting everyone in your organization to buy into and commit to your game plan requires a good deal of salesmanship. It is not enough to simply lay out what you expect your people to do for you, you need to convince them that the relationship is a synergistic one and that there are real-world benefits for them to realize if they will trust you and make the commitment necessary. Unless they see a reason for them to put themselves on the line for you—whether it's on the playing field or in the office—they will never give you the level of intensity that you need from your people in order to succeed in this hyper-competitive world.

And that's what I have always looked for in my people: intensity.

Showing up during the course of normal business hours and simply completing those assignments given to them doesn't do a damn thing for me. And, in the long run, it doesn't do anything for them either.

They may wear business casual instead of helmets and pads, but I want my people to come to work each and every day ready to give me, themselves, and our company absolutely everything that they've got. I'm looking for people who will play no matter what, who will play until they're absolutely exhausted, puke on my shoes, and then get right back to executing on the jobs that they've been assigned. (All right, maybe not puke on my shoes, but you get the idea.)

There's no easy way to achieve anything worthwhile in this world and that type of absolute commitment from your people is no exception. If you want that sort of dedication from your people day-in and day-out, then you have to show them as much (or lots more) every single day yourself. You have to lead by example and let them all know that no one believes in your vision more than you do and no one is running harder to chase it down and make it real.

Today, my company has more than 200,000 employees and there have been well over a million people when you consider all of the security officers I have employed throughout my career. With so many people having worked for me over the years, I can absolutely state unequivocally that not one of them ever worked harder than I did. Not one.

Did some work as hard as I did? I hope every one of them did. But I have never had an employee that's worked harder than me, not only because I would see that as a failure in myself, but more importantly I would view that as a betrayal of the unspoken promise I have made to each and every one of them, to the commitment that I have made to them.

This is how I live and work. I know my team recognizes this and responds in kind. Everyday.

That's why we have been able to achieve a level of success that every expert told me was impossible and that's why our company was recently recognized in 2017 by *Forbes* magazine as one of the best places to work.

Once you have the game plan in place and your people have committed to it, you need the most talented team possible to actually execute on it. Bill Walsh and Bill Belichik were football geniuses, but they needed gifted players to turn all of those Xs and Os into wins and championships.

First and foremost, managing a team or an organization is tough work and it requires making hard decisions on a regular basis. No coach likes to cut a kid and no CEO wants to have that conversation that concludes with one of their people packing their office into a box and going home. Sometimes, however, it just needs to be done.

That being said, anyone who's not buying into the game plan, anyone who's creating distractions in the locker room, those miscreants and malcontents are a cancer to the organization and they have to be cut out swiftly and completely or their discord will spread and infect the entire body of the organization. If someone's not 110 percent all in, then they have to be cut loose.

I look at my employees and grade them A, B, and C. The A's are your top performers and they need a degree of input and positive reinforcement, but basically, they're self-directed. You can put them in any situation that comes up and you can count on them to stick to the game plan and execute with everything that they've got. They're easy to manage.

The C's are easy to manage, too. The C's aren't getting the job done and haven't demonstrated an interest in improving themselves and their performance. It's easy to let them go off in another direction and allow them the freedom to see if they can't find a better situation elsewhere. It's the right thing to do for both of you.

The B's are the team members that require the most skill in managing. I call them The Killer B's because in many instances they can kill your organization. Or make it.

There are fifty-three positions on a professional football team and not one of those slots has room for any level of mediocrity. In the same way, there shouldn't be a single position within your organization that isn't an absolute necessity to your company's overall performance and, because of that, there is no room for mediocrity in any of those jobs.

With your Killer B's, you either have to manage them up or you have to manage them out. By that, I mean that if you have a B employee, then it's your (or your team's) responsibility to determine what the problem is and help them get to that A level.

Do they need a little bit more coaching until they gain experience? Is there some disconnect between the two of you on job responsibilities?

Whatever the problem may be, I think you owe it to the employee and to the larger organization to give everyone the opportunity to develop themselves into an A-level employee. But that's the important part right there: they have to be willing to put in the work. If there's a B-level employee who won't respond to the effort given to coach them up to the A level, then to my way of thinking that's just an overperforming C-level employee and I've already made it clear what has to happen to those C-level people.

The final component necessary to become a great leader is honesty, but by that I mean more than simply telling the truth.

Facts are facts. Reality *is*. There's no escaping any of that and nothing to be gained by ignoring, either.

When I talk about honesty as an essential quality that every leader must possess, exhibit, and cultivate, I mean not only truthfulness, but also being open to and receptive to "the truth" as others see it.

We all see this world in different ways. While you may be committed to your own point of view, that sort of self-assurance can quickly mutate into self-deception and a level of arrogance that can be disastrous to any organization. For example, if your game plan has a flaw in it that the other team has discovered and is taking advantage of, you have to listen to the players out on the field who tell you about the adjustments that the other team is making. More than that, you have to have a healthy relationship with your people and encourage an environment in which they feel safe and comfortable to come to you and tell you the truth, especially when you might not want to hear it.

Because of that, when I talk about honesty in this respect, I am also including the ability to put your ego in your pocket. Every one of us has an ego. (I may have a little one myself.) But everyone also knows that the ego is never a 100 percent reliable reflection of ourselves or our situations. In order to be completely honest in your communications with your team, you need to be able to put your ego aside and welcome a differing perception that maybe suggests that you're misinformed or simply wrong about a situation. You have to be able to table your ego and consider those suggestions honestly and without the interference of the need to save face.

Be aware that sometimes the voice that's saying all the things you don't want to hear is your own. Sometimes the one who has the best insight into the situation and has uncovered the flaws in your plan is none other than your own inner-critic. You need to be strong enough to listen to that voice as well.

I had a game plan. Things aren't going the way I thought they would. What do I need to change?

Those are, I think, the personal qualities that are most necessary to being a good leader.

Once you've identified and devoted yourself to their development—you have to get better and better, every day—I think you also need to wrap your head around the fact that even with the greatest achievements that you may realize in business, there is no finish line. Ever.

The same is true for most endeavors, including football.

Bill Belichick. Chuck Noll. Don Shula—There's a long line of head coaches in the NFL who were genius strategists and proficient coaches at getting the most out of everyone on their team. But I can guarantee you that there's never been a Super Bowl-winning coach who didn't sit down with the film the very next day and start to analyze that game in terms of what they needed to improve on in the coming season.

There is no finish line to greatness. It never ends.

You have to have the ability and the endurance as a CEO and as a leader to continue to bring that same level of commitment and passion every single day, year after year after year. Great leaders have the ability to dig deep and find that stamina to continue to do all of the things they need to be successful, to drive and push the organization towards its goals.

And that doesn't mean displaying perseverance only in the face of the stinging losses that are unavoidable to everyone. It is just as important to maintain that intensity in the glow of your greatest success. You cannot allow yourself to be lulled into a satisfied sense of complacency no matter what it is you think you have achieved.

You have to go hard. Every. Damn. Day. The foot can never come off of the accelerator. The reason is right there in our (not-so-distant) history.

Blockbuster Video is my favorite example. They went into a mom-and-pop industry and just devastated it. In a very short period of time, they took over the home entertainment industry and set up a retail store on what seemed like every corner.

And then Netflix happened.

When Netflix first made their appearance in the market, they weren't streaming content yet, they were a service that required you to fill out an order and they'd send you a video in a couple days, hardly the instant gratification that Blockbuster offered its customers. The Netflix scheme didn't seem like a competitor to the mighty Blockbuster who had warehouses of videos, distribution facilities around the country, and all of the assets necessary to completely destroy Netflix at their own game. But they didn't.

Instead of responding to the threat, instead of seeing the potential to grow their business even bigger, instead of offering their customers an even better service, Blockbuster simply rested on its laurels and laughed at the competition. The rest, as they say, is history.

All of a sudden Netflix took advantage of developing technology (technology that had been equally available to Blockbuster) and several years later they've become the absolute definition of excellence in home entertainment with more than 100 million subscribers, while Blockbuster (once a publicly traded company) is now just the punchline to a very bad joke.

I don't care how successful a company is, every day is a battle and you better be committed to reloading and answering that challenge or I guarantee you that you will fall to it.

You have to constantly be moving forward. You have to be looking to emerging technologies, examining potential partnerships, opening new markets. You have to have your eye on a future that is substantially greater than your current state or you will stagnate, stall, and then fail.

That's one of the greatest challenges that any leader faces. You have to keep yourself motived and, even more important, you have to keep your people motivated and fully engaged because continuing to be successful when you're on top and everyone is gunning for you is even harder than climbing your way to that peak in the first place.

As the game gets bigger and bigger, it gets harder and harder and harder. The stakes are greater, the competition is more focused. There are more and more moving pieces. Where before there may have been a dozen issues that you had to keep your eye on, now there are hundreds of them—and any one of them could be a disaster if not handled the right way. Every quarter those past results disappear (no matter how much you exceeded all reasonable expectations) and people stand back and dare you to get over the next hurdle, climb to the next summit.

In a really odd sort of way, once you get to a certain level of success, once you're no longer "the little guy," you lose all of the advantages of being the underdog. All of a sudden, you're Goliath, not David. And I promise you that if Goliath doesn't bring his "A game" every damn day, then no matter how big he may be, he will fall.

That means taking care of your customers, from your largest marquee names to your smallest mom-and-pop client. You have to be focused on providing better service than you did the day before. You have to make the most of every opportunity to grow. And you have to keep your people always motivated.

You have to be your best you … because that's what a leader does.

CHAPTER 40
Move Forward

Moving forward from Universal Protection's merger with Allied-Barton was no small job. Integration meant identifying all of the potential synergies and maximizing those rewards. It meant rebranding every single office, every one of our uniformed service providers, all of our materials. Everything.

At the same time that all of this was happening, I was giving my initial presentations to the Allied-Barton teams, welcoming them into our family and explaining our vision and our expectations. I was also going out and visiting customers that had previously been served by Allied-Barton and explaining to them our continued commitment to providing the very best service in the industry.

Within six months of the merger being announced, we had fully integrated and consolidated all of the offices.

We had rebranded every single uniform in the company. This wasn't a situation in which we could simply slap a Universal patch on the uniforms of those guards who had previously served with the company we acquired or put new lettering on the fleet of company cars. This time around it meant rebranding every single uniform and each vehicle in the entire (new) company across the United States, Canada, Puerto Rico, and the US Virgin Islands. Everyone and everything had to get new Allied-Universal insignias.

We had to rebrand and redecorate all of the offices and republish all of the point-of-sales materials in our system. Everything had to be reworked and rebranded to reflect our new identity.

We took the next six months to concentrate on the back office. That step required us to rework our accounts and billing to create a totally integrated system that would be best for our customers, whom we were aware were undergoing a transition of their own. The focus here was to assure every client that there would be no disruption in the level of excellent service that they had always received.

In business, it is not unusual for a merger to take two years or more to create the sort of synergies that the parties had hoped to create through their union. It is even more common, however, for the merger to fall apart completely and for those shared efficiencies to fall by the wayside without ever being realized.

I'm pleased and proud to say that this has not been the case for the Allied-Barton-Universal merger. (And I was always aware that there were many observing us who were convinced that we would never be able to work things out and come out of the merger with a company that fulfilled the promise of two giants working as one.)

While I exceeded even my own demanding work schedule in order to play my part in facilitating this harmonious situation, much of the credit for the success of our merger is owed to the CEO of Allied-Barton.

Prior to the merger, we had been friendly rivals. (As I've said previously, although this is a multi-billion-dollar industry, it is in many ways a small town in which everyone knows everyone else.) Going into the merger, I wasn't 100 percent certain how he was going to react—particularly because I had felt that there was some personal motivation in the two scuttled acquisition attempts and our anticlimactic Memphis meeting. Once the papers were signed, however, he went immediately from competitor to partner.

He graciously said to me, "I'm getting out of your way. I'll help you with anything that you need. Feel free to come to me with any questions that you have along the way." He was just an absolute gentleman about everything and I think that spirit of focusing on the company and our clients above any other consideration was very much the spirit that made this merger as effective as it has been. He has transitioned onto the board and continues to be an invaluable partner and contributor.

And so, within the course of a single year, we had created Allied-Universal. This was unquestionably the absolute dominant force in the security industry with revenues in excess of $5 billion at that time, although today Allied Universal's revenues are greater than $7 billion annually.

It is, quite simply, the best. Large enough to serve the most demanding client needs and yet attention-detailed so that it still caters to every single customer's individual security requirements.

It is everything I had ever hoped it could be. Everything I had dreamed it would be.

I had kept that promise. I had made my dream come true.

I thought back to my meeting in the executive dining room just before I left BFI to take that job at Universal. I remembered all the promises I had made to myself about going out and making a billion-dollar company of my own.

I had kept that promise. I had made my dream come true.

CHAPTER 41
Don't Slow Down

Of course, fulfilled promises and realized dreams are no reason to slow down.

While we were still negotiating with Allied-Barton, I was in talks to acquire a number of other companies. Again, my private equity partners were a little surprised. "Steve, you've made all of these acquisitions. Maybe after the Allied-Barton and Universal merger is settled, you should take a break and wrap your arms around what you've taken on."

I couldn't help but think about the hundreds of conversations I had had with Brian over the exact same subject. "No. We've worked too hard to set up these other companies. They're both great companies and if we don't pick them up, someone else will. And I'm not about to let that happen." Again, there wasn't much of a debate after that.

So, while we merged with Allied-Barton in August of that year, in September we acquired an $80 million company out of the Northeast. And in October we acquired a $300 million company, also from the Northeast.

Of course, each of these acquisitions took a tremendous amount of time, effort, and energy. But by this time, my team were all field-tested experts in the whole long, difficult process. From the VP of acquisitions to our legal team, everyone from operations and human resources, everyone played their part in integrating these huge businesses into our own.

Despite the fact that we were in the midst of the largest merger the industry had ever seen, I knew it was important not to let up on our vision to continue growing the company. We continued to grow on that same trajectory both in terms of our organic sales growth and also through important acquisitions in the industry.

In early 2018, we acquired another $100 million company. We continue to be laser-focused on improving as a company, both in terms of the services we provide to our existing customers and our unending quest to continue to grow our company through an aggressive acquisition practice.

Ernest Hemingway once wrote, "There is nothing noble in being superior to your fellow man; true nobility is being superior to your former self." I think that's true for any individual, but I think it's also equally applicable to a company.

I don't at all measure the company we are today against any of the achievements we've made over the years. Instead, I choose to look to the future, I continue to be focused on making the company not just bigger, but better. More efficient. More everything.

My focus is on creating the indisputable giant of the industry, the largest and best provider of security services not just today, but into tomorrow. We're committed to being on the bleeding edge of the amazing breakthroughs that are now being made with next-generation technology. We are searching for every possible way that we can improve the services that we provide our customers.

It's not necessarily a complicated or sophisticated company philosophy: deliver the best service in the industry to our clients. That might not be worthy of a Harvard Business School study, but it worked out pretty well for a little family-owned company in Southern California not so long ago.

CONCLUSION
No Off Season

While I was working on this project, someone asked me if writing this book had led me to ever think about the seven-year-old version of me who had set up shop with his homemade shoe shining kit on the streets of Livermore, California.

I smiled, because it's all too easy for me to remember that little kid. I remember him—and that experience—so well, because my attitude has never really changed. When I marched down to that corner, I only had one thing on my mind: being the best. Even if that meant surpassing my father's bold boasts about the shoeshine boy that he had been at my age.

When I became involved in football, it was the same way for me. Of course, I wanted to win every game that I ever played—as badly as anyone I've ever lined up with or against—but from the very first time I ever put on a helmet and pads, I was also able to see beyond just what was happening there on the field over the course of sixty minutes. Football was always something much more to me than just a game and, I think, that's why I was able to not only compete at the high level that I always played at, but also to endure all of the hardships, sacrifices, and near-constant pain that it necessitated to be the kind of player that I expected myself to be.

As a result, I never thought in terms of one particular game or another. The final tick of the clock was never the end of anything for me. Instead, it signified the beginning of a period to review the game just concluded so that I could learn from both my successes and failures, to train myself to improve my performance, and to ensure that when the next game day rolled around I was the most prepared guy on that field—on *any* field.

I brought that same mentality with me when I began my career in business. Whether it was landing my very first job right out of school or signing on the dotted line to finalize the latest multi-million-dollar acquisition, I have never been one to celebrate a deal. That's not because I don't appreciate each individual achievement—believe me, I recognize every single day how incredibly fortunate I have been (and am) to work with the amazing team that surrounds me—but just like when I was playing football, my mind is simply focused on reviewing my most recent performance, bettering myself accordingly, and then stepping back into the board room as the best-prepared, most-focused guy at the table.

I'm aware that some people my mistake this attitude for a lack of satisfaction with what I have achieved at these various levels in my life. I assure you that nothing could be further from the truth. In fact, it's the exact opposite. I'm extremely grateful for everything I have achieved and it's that sense of gratitude that leaves me hungry for more. And by "more," I'm not speaking about money or any of the other trappings that people often think are markers of success, but which have never really played any sort of motivating role for me. Instead, I'm talking about my expectations for myself, as a businessman, as a leader, and as a man.

I will always get up every morning and expect more of myself than I did the day before. That's just how I'm hardwired. It's in my DNA. And I'll tell you, I'm grateful for that.

I'm grateful for all of the challenges I had to face. The tragic string of injuries that I faced as a teen and young adult crushed my dreams of playing in the NFL, but they didn't crush me. Instead, they taught me to rise above the sort of disappointments that too many people let limit their entire lives. With the advantageous perspective of time, I can say now that if I had made it all the way to the NFL, I never would have reached the heights that I have attained in my current business career.

I'm grateful for every crappy hotel I had to stay in while we grew our company because we didn't have the money for me to stay some place where I didn't have to shore up the door with a chair propped under the doorknob. Those experiences, as trying as they were at the time, only served to fuel my fire to reach a point in my career where those considerations would no longer exist for me—and they make me appreciate absolutely every night I now spend in a Ritz-Carlton. I'm grateful for every financial crisis I weathered, because all of those trying times gave me an insight into my business, this industry, and the world of finance that I wouldn't have had if circumstances hadn't forced me to look so deeply for some viable option for our company to survive and grow.

I'm grateful for everyone who has played a part in this story. Not just the many people who supported my vision and assisted me along the way. I'm grateful for the doubters and the haters and the competitors too, because every one of them forced me to become stronger and sharper.

So, when I talk about always looking forward to the next challenge and success, it's not ingratitude speaking, just the opposite. It's a philosophy about being grateful for what I have but demanding more from myself.

Once in a while someone will suggest to me that this personal philosophy must necessarily lead to a feeling of perpetual disappointment. That is, if there's never enough, then I must never be satisfied. They couldn't be further off of the mark. In my mind, there is no greater satisfaction than exceeding what you reasonably thought you were capable of doing, in pushing yourself harder and getting results that are greater than your dreams.

That to me is the secret to happiness.

When I was much younger, I thought my attitude was just how you needed to play football. When I moved on from there and was first starting in business, I thought that this outlook was simply the spirit of success.

As an older, more experienced, and more mature man, however, I can see now that football and even business were never the game, they were (and are) merely components of a larger contest: the game of life.

> **In my mind, there is no greater satisfaction than exceeding what you reasonably thought you were capable of doing, in pushing yourself harder and getting results that are greater than your dreams.**

In the end, while I have certainly offered much of my outlook in football-based metaphors, this isn't a book about football. While I am absolutely confident that any reader of these pages could incorporate the lessons that I have laid out into their own careers and benefit from them accordingly, this isn't a business book either. Not really.

This is a book about life. And for me, football and business have just been really important subjects in that greater work. But that's all they've been.

The real game—the only one that matters when "the big clock" ticks all the way down—is life. I see that now.

And more importantly, that insight has only intensified my determination to continue to strive for excellence and to push myself to surpass even those seemingly impossible standards. Every night when I finally go to bed, I find I can never sleep (ever) because my mind is racing over the events of the day, "watching film" of every interaction and transaction from that day with the intention of finding ways to better myself.

As a CEO and business leader and as a friend, a mentor, and a member of my community, I see every opportunity I have to improve other people's lives and, in so doing, to enrich my own.

I review (and cherish) every moment I get to spend with my wife and sons, because I want always to be a better husband, a better father; to be the man that they deserve. So, I will absolutely fly half-way around the world at the drop of a hat if a deal or an operation needs me there, but I always make certain that I am home when I am needed. And I make sure that I am always right there on the sidelines to keep the promise that my father made to me when he told me that my proudest moments in life would be when my own boys took that field—and, you know what? My old man was absolutely right. As always.

Life is the game, my friends.

There are goals and rules and teammates (and opponents.) There are hardships to be endured, challenges to overcome, and glory to be won. And there is a clock that is always counting down on us.

My strong advice, the very last piece that I'll offer you here, is to give that game absolutely everything that you've got. Leave everything that you've got out on the field and come back every day more focused and more determined than ever. Make your opportunities, pocket your ego, and play both sides of the ball *and* special teams. Take every snap and play absolutely every down like the entire game depended on it, because in a way it does.

Life is the game, my friends.

And in that game, there really is no off season.

A Special Offer from ForbesBooks

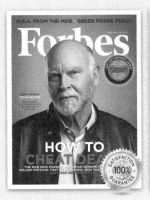  

Other publications bring you business news. Subscribing to *Forbes* magazine brings you business knowledge and inspiration you can use to make your mark.

- Insights into important business, financial and social trends
- Profiles of companies and people transforming the business world
- Analysis of game-changing sectors like energy, technology and health care
- Strategies of high-performing entrepreneurs

Your future is in our pages.

To see your discount and subscribe go to Forbesmagazine.com/bookoffer.

Forbes